Advance Praise for

"The villains and heroes Moran bring [...] a video game involving deer hunters and street warfare. The fact that these are true stories involving leaders only make the stories more compelling. A great read, full of lessons about contemporary organizations."
—Greg Ballard, Senior Vice President, Digital Games,
    Warner Bros Interactive Entertainment
    Former CEO, GluMobile

"Rich Moran is the Will Rogers of the business world. He's a highly experienced and credentialed professional and also a witty humorist, as oxymoronic as those two things might sound. If there were such a thing as business vaudeville, Rich would be its star attraction. He has a gift for pointing out the absurdities of organizational life that is at once tragically funny and funnily tragic. He's got a wry, down-home style, a very keen eye for the bizarre details of the office, and he loves poking fun at executives, especially CEOs, but in a way that makes even them laugh out loud. Seriously. *Sins and CEOs* is his funniest, most poignant, and instructive book yet. Instructive because each of his tales includes some serious morals at the end, and they really do teach important lessons. Rich's anecdotes will entertain you on your next plane trip across the country and back, but you'd better keep a tight hold on the book. Your seat mate will try to steal it from you, because you're having too good a time reading it. I know these are tough times and we ought to be terribly serious about business, but you really must take the time to read this book. It'd be a sin if you didn't."
—Jim Kouzes, coauthor of the bestselling *The Leadership Challenge*

"I can think of a few hundred CEOs who will read this book to see if they are guilty as charged. I can think of a few thousand CEOs who could benefit from reading this book. I can think of a few million careers that could be improved by paying attention to Moran's ideas on avoiding sins."
—J. David Martin, former Chairman & CEO
    Young Presidents Organization (YPO)

"*Sins and CEOs* is a fun, easy read. Moran "double clicks" on the critical lessons so we can learn how to avoid the common pitfalls. It's not easy to navigate the choppy waters of being the CEO, and since we are all at least the CEO of our own careers, everyone should read this book to avoid the sinful temptations."

—Ed Colligan, Former CEO of Palm, Inc.

"Rich Moran writes about company leaders with insight and humor. The accuracy in *Sins and CEOs* will make you laugh and cry at the same time. This compendium of how to avoid human frailty will inspire you to become a more effective person and to help others around you do the same."

—Jeffrey Pfeffer, Professor, School of Business, Stanford University
    Author of *Power: Why Some People Have It—and Others Don't*

"*Sins and CEOs* invites us inside the head of a seasoned professional with startling observational skills. Rich Moran looks at the complex problems faced by real CEOs, and challenges us to consider simple yet powerful leadership solutions. *Sins* is really funny, but sharp enough to cut through our human tendency to avoid the truth."

—David K. Mensah, Principal Partner
    DKBWAVE Training and Consulting

SINS *and* CEOs

Other Books by Richard A. Moran

Never Confuse a Memo with Reality
Beware Those Who Ask for Feedback
Cancel the Meetings, Keep the Doughnuts
Fear No Yellow Stickies
Nuts, Bolts and Jolts

SINS *and* CEOS

Lessons from Leaders and Losers

That Will Change Your Career

Richard A. Moran

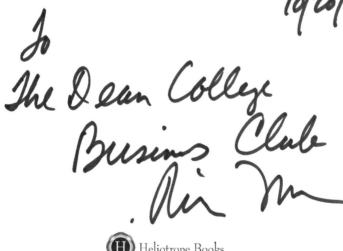

 Heliotrope Books
New York

Heliotrope Books LLC
c/o SB Design
125 East 4th Street
New York, NY 10003

Designed and Typeset by Naomi Rosenblatt with AJ&J Design
Cover concept by Richard A. Moran
        Designed by Naomi Rosenblatt, Judith Rosenblatt and AJ&J Design
        Thanks to Dr. Belle Wiggins for letting us burn org charts in her fireplace.

To those heroes
who present this book to all the jerks,
clowns and weirdos who should read it, but won't,
I promise I will keep writing.

To my family,
Carol, Brady, Scott, Megan and John,
I dedicate this book in the hopes
that we will all avoid sins.

"Uneasy lies the head that wears a crown."
—William Shakespeare, *Henry IV*

Contents

About the Author

Richard Moran is a nationally known authority on corporate leadership and workplace issues. He is a venture capitalist, former executive at software companies and a former Accenture partner where he worked in media and entertainment, communications and technology. His clients have included News Corporation, AT&T, Apple, Hewlett Packard, American Airlines and Oracle. He is credited with creating the genre of "business bullet" books, based on the premise that business is often best directed by simple, rather than complex principles. He is the Vice Chair at Accretive Solutions and serves as a director on several boards.

Moran's previous books include: National Bestseller *Never Confuse a Memo with Reality*; *Beware Those Who Ask for Feedback*; *Fear No Yellow Stickies*; *Cancel the Meetings, Keep the Doughnuts*; and, *Nuts, Bolts and Jolts*. He has appeared on CNN, NPR, CNBC and in *Fortune*, the *Financial Times* and other media discussing change and leadership. His radio show "In the Workplace" runs weekly on KCBS. He is the President of Moran Manor & Vineyards and lives in San Francisco with his wife and four children.

Author's Note

Hard as it might be to believe, the stories in this book are true. On occasion I exercised the author's prerogative to make the vignette more understandable or to provide a lesson with a fairy-tale ending. Company and CEO names are kept private to protect individuals, share prices, and my future employment. Guessing is welcome but names won't be revealed. Any relation between the names used in the book and any real CEO is purely coincidence.

The number of successful CEOs who are women grows every day. I have enjoyed working with some of them and know their road to success is more difficult than a man's. Last time I looked, however, the vast majority of CEOs were still men. As of this printing, only three percent of the Fortune 500 had women CEOs, so I am taking the author's prerogative and using the masculine pronoun to avoid the cumbersome "he or she" construct throughout. Think of it as a gentle means to keep women CEOs away from sins.

—RAM

Foreword

It's always with trepidation that I look forward to Rich Moran's next book. He never fails to hit the "Yes!" button when it comes to nailing the travails and disappointments of the workplace. He cheers me when he honestly describes the pain and agony so many experience, and relates it back to flawed leaders. And he always succeeds in making me look harder at myself, questioning my own leadership behaviors, and what I need to do or stop doing. He digs into each leader's self perceptions, holding up the mirror of truth. It puts me on notice. I'm sure it does many others as well.

Here's a paradox we face in the workforce: We grow up absorbing the vibrations of democratic culture where we're all equally important, vital citizens. If we have functioning parents, and fortunately most of us do, we're encouraged to be who we are and do what we choose. Years of schooling further develop the democratic principles of equality and individual opportunity that we will enjoy throughout our lives. School curricula enable us to become educated and autonomous, if we take advantage of the occasion. Fortunately, most of us do. Those who go on to college or graduate school avail ourselves of higher learning that will enhance our range of professional opportunities.

Then we transition to the workplace, where our first manager can frame our attitudes and expectations for decades to come. Subsequent managers reinforce or contradict that impression, depending on their difference from (or similarity to) that first manager. Whatever the case, we go from thriving, independent and self-actualizing young citizens to low-person-on-the-totem-pole of an anti-democratic hierarchy, supervised by an authoritarian autocrat. He who hires also fires. His absolute control and authority over what, how, when, why, where and who in the workplace takes command of our lives, turning us either inside out, or upside down.

I can't forget my first job and boss. He put me in a storage closet, which everyone accessed, on a stool with a table. I was to analyze a giant toilet paper box full of computer print-outs which had been gathering dust for six months. He said, "We're a little hard up for space, hope you don't mind. You have six months to analyze and interpret all this data." Except that I didn't. Three weeks later he came back to say we need the final analyses in sixty days, probably less—be ready.

There was no mention of break or lunch schedule, nor a discussion of normal work hours. The message was you have a job to do; it's your first job. How well you perform will determine your next job, and so on. In a quiet moment of poking around the storage closet I found the organization guide. I counted twelve layers between me and the CEO. As my closet was also in the basement of a building, I realized that, for all the glory and honor of completing my graduate education and achieving my first professional placement with a truly great company, I couldn't be lower than a snake belly. Would this be the end, or the beginning, of my self-actualizing journey? With a combination of great and good leaders who encouraged democratic involvement in the business, and mediocre and outright bad leaders who took it away, I climbed the ladder until I was the leader, first of Shell's global HR function and then of the company's largest subsidiary, Shell Oil Company.

Throughout my career I felt and saw the sins that Rich describes. I also committed many along the way. We're not perfect, we humans, no matter how hard we try. Some of the best advice I received, apart from that offered by impressive leadership development programs, came from subordinates. It tended to sound like this: "Don't forget us, the little people; we make or break you." "You'll always have to put your shoes on one at a time, just like I do." "The atmosphere at the top is thin, but don't let it affect your judgment."

With empathy that never borders on indulgence, Rich Moran presents the opportunities and the dilemmas of leaders. He backs his discussion with real examples that are sad and true. Since we met years ago and worked together on leadership development in the 1990's, I've been a direct beneficiary of his unique insight into workplace dynamics. I've also been privy to his examples of both extraordinary and disastrous leadership behaviors. In this book he shares a thriving inventory of characters he's worked with. Somehow, he's managed to translate their follies and foibles into gifts for the reader.

In short, *Sins and CEOs* captures the lessons learned from leaders and losers and provides us with memorable summaries or "takeaways." Metaphorically, Rich provides backbone braces for wafflers and cowards, vibrators and cow prods for fiddlers and the paralyzed, and software patches for the clueless. Those are remedies for the passive sinners. For the active sinners, he ratchets up the corrective aids. Armor-piercing medicated arrows are reserved for the arrogant and vain; lubricated brain-changing bullets will transform, or remove, the fibbers and assholes. He covers the waterfront of learning from learners while teaching the unteachable.

Everyone should come away from reading *Sins and CEOs* with a greater sense of his or her own humanity, with humility and renewed commitment to prevail. Leaders who choose not to sin will encourage honor, democratic participation and interaction between their team members. And those who motivate their workforce shall reap the results.

John Hofmeister
Founder and CEO of Citizens for Affordable Energy
Former CEO of Shell Oil

Introduction

In recent times, CEOs have been much in the news, much to their embarrassment. They are on the front page of non-business magazines and newspapers every day, sometimes in handcuffs. They are key talking points in presidential press conferences. They are discussed around the kitchen table and on the floor of the U.S. Congress. They are vilified for making too much money and sanctified for saving corporations and jobs. They are human; they are our neighbors. They are all around us in airports or on the street, yet most of us do not come into direct contact with them. They are the chairs of the local symphonies and ballets, but they are criticized for not caring about the arts or culture. They are very public and very private and generally hard to characterize as a group. They are expected to have big egos, but when they're ruled by their egos, they are criticized. The CEO sets the flavor and the agenda for his organization, for better or worse.

I've worked with hundreds of CEOs. As a longtime consultant and partner at Accenture and through work at Accretive Solutions, I've consulted for CEOs and tried to sell them big projects. I deal with CEOs every day, trying to get them to buy or fund companies, and to invest in technologies. They visit me regularly and give presentations in the hopes that I will invest millions in their idea or company. By far, they are a highly motivated, highly compensated, and talented group of people. But sometimes I see a CEO acting badly or exercising poor judgment and wonder if he took stupid pills.

CEOs BEHAVING BADLY: DIRTY FINGERNAIL CLIPPINGS

Clawing his way to the top was my friend Sam's goal in life. The "clawing" would soon take on new meaning for Sam.

Sam desperately wanted to be a CEO: he went to the right MBA program, read every biography of Steve Jobs, took all the hardest assignments in the company, and moved his family around the world at great emotional expense to his wife and children. Finally, it happened. Sam was promoted and took over the big corner office. So what if it wasn't a huge company like IBM or Procter and Gamble. He had made it. He was a capital C, capital E, capital O!

Sam inherited the corner office and fancy desk of the former CEO and, because he wanted to send out the message that he was cost-conscious, he decided to keep the perfectly good "old" desk. With pride, he decorated his desktop and included an arrangement of photos of the kids and the Lucite cubes of all his deals. But when he opened the top middle desk drawer where he hoped to house his collection of special Mont Blanc pens, he found, to his dismay, that all the little compartments were filled with fingernail clippings: souvenirs from the previous occupant. Aaargh. Gross!

It was a moment worthy of a barf, as Sam later described it. He ordered a new desk that day and he never talked to the old CEO again.

The first and overwhelming response to this story is: "Yuck! How could someone be such a pig?" But then the response moves to an even more critical sort: "How could someone be so cruel as to take away someone else's moment of triumph? Why didn't he just clean out his desk properly?"

THE DIRTY FINGERNAIL CLIPPINGS CHECKLIST

Leaving your fingernail clippings around for someone else to find sounds pretty bad, doesn't it? Before you react too strongly, think about just a few, similar workplace activities that might apply to you:

- Have you ever left a stack of dirty dishes in the company kitchen right under the sign that roars, "*Clean Up After Yourself! The Maids Are Gone.*"?

- While you were on your way to work have you ever told yourself, "*I'm not going to do anything today. I just don't feel like it.*"?

- Were you ever mean to a coworker or customer just because you could be? Did you have a temporary "asshole attack" and regret it later?

- Do you take the newspaper with you to the bathroom and stay there for a long time to hide from your co-workers?

- Do you spend all day on Facebook or Twitter or some other site when someone is paying you to do something else? Like your real job?

- Do you ever avoid the difficult emails you receive, afraid to address the tough issues?

If you answered yes to any of the above then you are no different from the guy who trimmed his nails all day and slid the clippings into the drawer. It's just a matter of degree. Big sins and little sins hurt you and your organization, regardless of your rank on the org chart.

The Unique Onus of Being the CEO

If we are all guilty—some of the time—of the sins I just outlined, why are CEOs singled out for all they do? Why are they more likely to commit sins and why are their sins in our faces and newspapers? Here are three reasons I want to write about the responsibilities, shortcomings, and triumphs specifically of CEOs rather than those of everyone else:

- CEO Geometric Ripple Effect: The sins of a CEO have a far-reaching wave effect. His actions may create ripples in the economy, the environment, and our daily lives. What he does (or doesn't do) affects employees, shareholders, the community, pensions, inheritances, families, and all the bowling leagues in town.

- CEO Clout: A CEO has the power to ruin someone's day with a casual comment or a weird glance. Conversely, a leader's stray or tasteless actions might damage or bring down the entire company.

- CEO Blindness: A CEO should be particularly self-aware, a good listener, and an excellent observer of human behavior. He should know if sins are being committed around him, even if no one will tell him. To miss the sins is to become the "emperor with no clothes," who, by the way, was the ultimate blind sinner until the little boy corrected him.

In short, CEOs are human, like all of us, and they are capable of committing sins that range from gross hygiene mistakes to major crimes. But leaders also bear the heavy responsibility of the entire organization. If the CEO doesn't succeed it will not only reflect on his record. His failure may kill the entire company and the careers of hundreds of people.

But it occurs to me too that CEOs are not "them." CEOs are us. We are all CEOs. Each of us, everyone of us is, at some level, the CEO of something. You may not be the CEO of General Electric, but you can be the CEO of your department or your neighborhood association or even your family.

At the most basic level, each of us is the CEO of our own life. We plan and guide our own careers, control our own actions and are accountable for our own results.

Unlike the rest of us, though, CEOs don't have as much room for committing sins—there is too much at stake. Their sins will lead them on the path to ridicule, or worse. For the rest of us, the sins could lead to not getting that raise or to getting dumped. At the very least, committing these sins will make us less successful.

And success is what this book is about—for the CEO and for you.

Of course, success means different things to different CEOs and that is often where the road to sin starts. To some it means improving share price and to others it means generating profits. To some it means building their individual track record and to others it means getting employees to like them. The sinner's path can truly be paved with a CEO's good intentions.

What This Book Is and Isn't About

This is not a treatise on the CEO as the biggest jerk in the world, or about the simple ways to be a good leader—that's all been done many times. Nor is it about etiquette or hygiene or how to succeed in your first 100 days. It is a book about the CEO you might know and see as he tries to do his job. And it's about what you can learn from his efforts, whether he succeeds or fails.

Nor is this a missive about the crimes of senior executives and how they have wrecked the economy or the environment or both. Far from it. I will not delve into the miasma of executive pay or those guys who are now in orange jumpsuits. Although some people are determined to perform in ways that make us scratch our heads and wonder, "What were they thinking?", most CEOs want to perform better and upgrade their organization or company. My hope is this book contributes to better behavior, better performance, and an understanding that we all commit sins.

So please do not expect hundreds of pages proclaiming, "My boss is an asshole." I don't believe that to be true. (After the publication of Robert Sutton's *The No Asshole Rule*, I feel we are all empowered to use that term in business books.) Most CEOs are not assholes, although there are more than a few for whom the term is apt, and they will be considered in some detail later.

Most business leaders are trying to do the right thing in a highly complicated world and trying to please many people, including Wall Street analysts who want a higher stock price, and their own families who want dad or mom to spend more time at home. In the hopes of meeting complex demands and expectations, all of us are likely to commit sins. But when a CEO commits sins, people might lose their jobs, the community might suffer, and people might go to jail—to name a few consequences.

I believe most leaders are doing their best every day to make their organizations successful. There are exceptions, and many of those are the ones in the headlines with a photo doing the "perp" walk. There are enough books about the leadership at Enron, WorldCom, Bear Stearns, Lehman Brothers, AIG, and BP. The stories here are often enough tales about those who are trying to do their best, but may be blind about the consequences of their actions and how they are perceived. Maybe hanging around with other executives has led some CEOs to believe that anything goes. Anything doesn't go.

CEOs are not bad people. Sometimes they just don't understand that their thoughtless, inelegant, or sinful actions may have drastic implications for everyone around them. And remember, we are all CEOs.

The CEO, in particular, seeks to avoid these sins for the sake of his career and the future of the organization. But none of us should succumb regularly to workaday temptations if we want to live a happy, successful, and balanced life. Regardless of our gender, personality, age, or Myers-Briggs type, we'd be well advised to take to heart these fateful lessons of the CEO.

As an observer and evangelist for change, I hope to point out those sins that we, along with our CEOs, are capable of committing and show the way to redemption. No doubt, some of us will continue to be sinners and suffer the consequences. I hope others will see the light I intend to shine in the following pages.

The lessons I describe here about CEOs behaving badly are the same stories that apply to all of us trying to make our way with success through our careers.

I hope, through these stories, to characterize the blind spots of leaders from my real-life experiences with them. And if any CEO reads this book, I hope he will glean lessons from it.

How to Use This Book

When I asked a batch of friends to name a sin that a CEO or leader might commit, the words "jerk," "ego," or "hubris" quickly rolled off the tongue. These words are synonyms for "aggression" and "attack." "Chainsaw Al" Dunlap of Sunbeam-Oster fame and others were labeled with these adjectives and wore them proudly. "Aggression" and the related sins it inspires are easy to spot. Other sins, much less easy to spot, that can invade your work life and wreak havoc are the "passive" sins. This book is organized into two parts that respectively address the passive and aggressive sins.

When reviewing the list of aggressive sins, it may be easy for you to say, "No way. I am not an asshole and I don't fib and I am not arrogant." But you might be caught short when you do the personal assessment on sins like waffling or inaction. In fact, that is how you can use the book: to ask yourself hard questions about the sins that are a little easier to hide and adjust. We are all guilty of some passive sins.

And since we are all guilty, I provide redemption for each sin in the form of prescriptions and takeaways. In keeping with the tone, the prescriptions are not complicated; they are more likely to be the converse of the sin. For example, if you are oblivious, you might need to pay attention to what is going on around you at work in new and more meaningful ways.

Sins are not bad news. Rather, they present opportunities to make changes. (Or you can leave the book on the CEO's chair at night.) Identifying problems, issues, and bad news is not the hard part of organizational life. The hard part is to make changes based on those assessments. I once had a very prominent CEO at a major company tell me, "I am not going to pay you a million dollars to tell me that we are f###ed up; I already know that. Start with what needs to change and what I need to do." The trajectory of the book is to shed new light on what you thought no one knew and then suggest the remedies.

CAREER TRAJECTORIES FOR THE CEO

Jokes and stories about our leaders today tend to portray them in less than glowing light. Some believe that there are three types of CEO:

1. The guy who founded something and grew it to the point where he could no longer make it successful and is waiting to be fired.

2. The guy who worked his way up through the map of the organization chart, understanding every process and strategy, until he got to the top and realized he didn't know what to do.

3. The guy who got lucky in the gene pool and inherited his role in spite of his talents.

There are talented and qualified leaders out there, and most do not fit into these three categories. But there is always room for improvement in a CEO, as there is for all of us.

These lessons about the antics of leaders apply to anyone in almost any situation. If you disappear from the job for five days like the former Governor of South Carolina did, chances are you will be fired. You can learn from leaders, whether you are the CEO of your family or a team. At work, you are probably the leader of a project or the field office or your sales territory. Michael Scott in the TV show *The Office* is the leader of the Scranton office and he is just as oblivious as some of the CEOs I describe here. As someone related to the show said, "If you don't know Michael Scott, you are Michael Scott." Some permutation of Michael Scott shows up throughout these chapters.

Part One

THE PASSIVE SINNER

(Sins of Omission)

1

THE SIN: COWARDICE

No Balls and Dangerous Meetings

"What an incompetent witch!" So says everyone that has to deal with the assistant to a notable CEO. "Why does he let her embarrass him like that?"

Ever wonder why some CEOs have terrible, insulting, and ineffective executive assistants? Could it be that they are afraid to fire them? Ever wonder why some leaders' communications to the employees, no matter how dramatic the environment, are just plain vanilla and bland? In fact, they don't ever say anything. Maybe these leaders are afraid to tell the truth and deal with the consequences.

Why do some CEOs surround themselves with handlers and PR people that form an impenetrable protective circle? Could it be because they fear dealing with the unknown or with unexpected conflict? We know these kinds of people—whether they are running a Fortune 500 company or the local YWCA.

One sin that can afflict all of us in the workplace is fear. If you think you have never been a coward at work, ask yourself just a few of these questions:

- Does the guy in the cube next to you smack his gum, clip his fingernails, or play on Facebook all day to the point of driving you crazy, but you ignore it?

- Does your boss leave yellow stickies on your computer screen saying "See me ASAP!" or "Redo the xxx spreadsheet!" instead of talking to you? And instead of communicating with him, do you show up every day scared to death of yellow stickies?

- Have you ever skipped over an email or a voice message because you were afraid of the content?

- Do you show up at "optional" work-related events like the company picnic even though you hate them, but you fear someone is taking attendance?

- Are you in constant fear of losing your job but don't look for another one because you are afraid your current boss will find out you are looking elsewhere and fire you?

- During your performance review, do you sit there silently while your manager glosses over your accomplishments and picks you apart for a minor weakness?

Sometimes being a coward at work is easier than dealing with an uncomfortable situation. While a little "grin and bear it" might be part of the workplace for all of us, a fearful or cowardly CEO is one that will burn in hell because he lacks the crucial power to fix things.

Any leader, man or woman, can appear macho. And any leader learned long ago that appearances can be more important than substance when it comes to exercising control. But there are always clues about a CEO's cowardice—telltale signs of a yellow streak running down his back. A big clue can often be found in what he avoids, including seemingly mundane activities such as facing a department that needs to trim costs.

A big energy company on the East Coast needed to cut cost—something that every company should know how to do by now. But like so many others, this company brought in consultants to do the work. (**First clue that the CEO is a coward: bringing in consultants to do dirty work like cutting costs.**) It was a top-to-bottom review of all department activities, and all groups were expected to make sacrifices. Part of my job as consultant was to deal with the finance/accounting departments, but the managers there kept stalling. They just would not meet with me. They probably hoped I would go away soon enough and all would be safe.

My dignity, my raise, and my plane ticket home depended on getting them to cooperate, so I was determined. Nonetheless, I just couldn't make them meet with me, and the project was incomplete until they did. The CEO defended them constantly, claiming they were always too busy with month-end, quarter-end, and annual reports, SEC filings, or something that had them "crazed." I never believed they were that busy because they came in late and left early, yet the CEO wouldn't put the press on them as he did on other groups.

There were suspicions that something weird was going on between the finance department and the CEO. I suspected he was afraid of the department because they could influence communication about company performance and stock price with a well-placed comment to the "Street."

In truth, the finance and accounting departments knew the purpose of our project better than anyone. They also knew that their own departments were fat, especially in management. They didn't want to participate in what they called "building their own coffin." Why work hard if you don't have to, they reasoned. After weeks of trying to get together with them, and with no help from the CEO, the meeting was finally scheduled on a beautiful fall evening during the department's annual off-site planning retreat.

The location was the company-owned rural resort in upstate New York, two hours away from headquarters and civilization. What I didn't know was that the date of the meeting was, coincidentally, the first day of deer-hunting season.

Driving by myself in a rental car, I was in a great mood—because the project was about to end. I had trouble following the map the company provided and half wondered why they were convening so far away from the office. The last turn was at a mile marker onto a dirt road, which made me wonder if I was in the right place. The dirt road went on for a rough few miles, and as I bumped through ditches and over boulders I swore to myself I would never buy a used rental car. The clocks had just reverted to standard time, so when I arrived in the early evening, it was the kind of pitch-black where you stand in place for a while waiting to get your bearings.

I could see the lights of the cabin, and I parked at the end of all the other cars in case I was in the wrong place. When I spotted a company sedan I knew I was in the right spot. I put on my navy-blue suit jacket, straightened my red paisley tie, picked up my laptop case, took a deep breath, and walked toward the building without being able to see where my feet were landing.

Guns and Accountants

As I got closer to the cabin I could hear classic Bruce Springsteen music, loud voices, and a lot of laughing. What I could also see as I neared the cabin were dead deer everywhere. They were hanging by their hind hooves on hooks in the ceiling of the porch, and some were strapped to the hoods of cars. Those deer that hadn't been strung up or strapped were stacked on top of each other on the porch floor. There must have been twenty of them, but the revelers had left a convenient path to the front door. Deer look a lot bigger and spookier when seen dead in the dark with their stomachs cut open and their eyes wide than when you see them grazing quietly on a hill.

These must not be regular accountants, I said to myself.

I looked to see if there were any of my consultant friends in the stack of dead animals and was relieved to see none. I knew no one in the group inside except for an occasional "hello" mumbled in the halls at headquarters. If I had any doubt why the CEO wouldn't deal with this group, I now knew for sure. He was afraid not only for the financial reports that the group might produce, he was afraid for his life. They had somehow intimidated him with their own macho swagger. These were not a set of timid accounting majors; these were people who knew they were riding a gravy train with biscuit wheels, and they really didn't want to change. The CEO was a coward and should have come down on them. Instead, he did nothing—and Beelzebub was taking notice.

Inside the cabin, there were no signs of a retreat. There were no easels with big pads of paper. There were no mission statements or lists of goals and objectives on the walls. There were no facilitators. They might have been killed already, I thought. There were only guns, whiskey, yelling, and loud music. The group was yukking it up while they were cleaning their rifles with long brushes and smelly rags. They were drinking whiskey straight from small glasses with no ice, and seemed half drunk. I hoped they were only half drunk. As I walked in, wearing my good blue suit, they welcomed me with enthusiasm and lots of slaps on the back. There were no women there, although the department was full of women clerks. The women probably did all the work in the department, I thought.

"We've been waiting for you," the director of internal auditing said. I promised myself not to tell any accountant or actuary jokes.

The group gave me a lot of credit just for being there and urged me to relax and have a shot or two with them. They laughed about the CEO not having the balls to cut any head count in their departments. "What a pussy," yelled out an accounts payable supervisor and everyone laughed as much at the CEO as at the AP guy.

The head of department put his arm around me and said, "Come on in and let's just chat—you, and all of us." At that point I knew I was faced with the choice of having the meeting with them right then, or maybe not ever having it. Another choice was to get whatever data I could from them and just make up the rest back at the office. These guys were sure we wouldn't have the meeting then and there. I was now sure that we would because the alternatives would keep me away from home longer.

THE "FAR SIDE" AT WORK

We had the meeting. We gathered around the fireplace in a semicircle without any guns or whiskey. I sat in the middle of the group, making sure that no one was behind me, and gathered the data I needed. And believe it or not, the group felt that they had contributed to making a better department. Even though the department would be smaller, the jobs would be better. They wanted to get rid of the "deadwood" in the department and had no difficulty pointing out all the waste and redundancy that had built up. One manager called his group the *"Office of Redundancy."* The group knew they were committing another sin, that of just plain being ineffective and they wanted to fix the problem. In effect, they had been waiting for someone to help them out of their sense of frustration that they couldn't change anything. I believed that they wanted things to change, but there were still those well-oiled guns and whiskey around.

At the end of the meeting, I left the cabin and went out into the pitch-black looking for my car. I had taken off my suit jacket and was wearing a white shirt, and I imagined a target on the back of it as in a Gary Larson "Far Side" cartoon. I could hear the clicking of gun parts as the managers resumed cleaning their guns. I thought I could hear some giggling too.

Driving back into town, I swore I would never wear a white shirt again and cursed the CEO. It was his job that should be eliminated. But the consolation was that his cowardice would destine him to hell.

WHAT WENT WRONG IN THE ENERGY COMPANY?

The energy company CEO was afraid that fragile alliances with the finance department would be jeopardized if he cut costs there. When any group senses fear in a CEO—be they employees, shareholders, the board of directors, or the competitors—it is time for the CEO to move on or end up in hell. The CEO in question did move on shortly after the dead deer incident and is no longer a CEO.

Why is it so difficult for some CEOs to deal with their own people, those same employees in the organization they are trying to govern? Do they not know that many organizational problems can best be solved by those closest to the work? Do they not realize that employees almost always know what's going on, and it is difficult to keep any secret from them? That's why no one believes Bernie Madoff acted alone in his huge Ponzi scheme. Employees almost always know what is going on in any organization, and if there are any cowards around, everyone will know who they are. What went wrong here is that the CEO was afraid that a finance or accounting manager would do something with the numbers to make him look bad.

It is not unusual for a CEO to insulate himself from the day-to-day activities of the business. Sometimes, the further he's removed, the greater his fear. It's too easy to enjoy the trappings of the corner office and grow detached from the real work. It's the first sign of the sin of cowardice: willingness to embrace the good life at the expense of the difficult work. We can all be guilty of the sin of cowardice—which might be better termed "avoidance"—depending on what we do. Avoiding the email with the information on your next assignment or the performance review for that poor performer fall in the same sin category. Cowardice and avoidance are the same sin; cowardice applies to the CEO, avoidance to the rest of us.

Why Are You Afraid of Your Incompetent Assistant?

A large technology company was suffering the same hard time as the rest of the economy in 2009. Based on cost-cutting data, the CEO made the decision at a staff meeting to eliminate three thousand jobs in China and a plant in Kansas City. The decision took less than five minutes. In the same meeting, a member of the executive committee mentioned that something needed to be done about the CEO's executive assistant. She was an embarrassment when it came to dealing with customers and didn't reflect well on the company. Everyone agreed, including the CEO, that she was incompetent and that the company "could do better," but the CEO deferred, saying, "She has been with me so long. I just can't bring myself to do it." As the staff left the room one muttered, "He just eliminated four thousand jobs around the world—the faceless employees—and we spent five minutes on it. Now he can't fire the incompetent that sits three feet from his office. What a coward."

All CEOs Should Have Big Ears

It may seem out of style and counterintuitive for leaders to consider, but they have much to learn from the "workers." I mean the real workers, like truck drivers and customer care agents and salespeople, because they are so damn honest. For many the honesty is directly related to the belief that, "I can say whatever I want because I probably have nowhere lower to go." When it comes to the CEO, this group will often say something like, "I'd like to see him do my job for just one day."

Sure, people are always worried about their jobs, but people at the bottom feel confident they will not lose their job if they tell the truth. Teamsters and others don't hold back very much when asked a question. Listening doesn't happen through surveys. Leaders who are really respected are not afraid to get out there and listen. A big part of President Obama's initial popularity was his willingness to get out of Washington and listen. Leaders who listen can learn, and don't we all say we want to be in a "learning organization"?

THE TRUCKING COMPANY: THROWING ROCKS ON STEREOS

The CEO of a large trucking company didn't feel comfortable going into the busy truck terminals that were distributed all across the country. You know those terminals, where the real work for the customers is done. Rather, he stayed in the corporate offices. Once again, consultants were brought in to deal with the people and the problems in the terminals. I led the consulting team that was trying to make the truck drivers and warehouse workers more productive. More importantly, there needed to be a way to motivate the workers to stop breaking the freight the trucks were trying to deliver. The freight was being smashed–literally. The company was paying so much in damaged freight that they had moved from being profitable to losing bundles of money every quarter. No one could figure out the problem of why so much was getting broken—or they were afraid to speak the truth.

The support of the forklift operators, the truck loaders, and all others involved was going to be the key to solving the problem. In this case, the teamsters had the answers and they knew it. The question was whether or not they would tell anyone, especially a consultant like me and my team. The CEO was sure they wouldn't talk or help with a solution to the problem. He avoided the problem for fear of what the solution might be.

I set up a meeting with some truck terminal workers.

"Whenever the 'suits' show up, it's not good for us," said one guy as I sat across from him. I was wearing a suit. "It always means do more with less and that we need to change some attitudes around here. Sometimes we like to show that others need to change attitudes too." He was eyeing my suit.

There was a group sitting around us listening and they started to snicker. The week before, they had locked two junior consultants in the trailer of an eighteen wheeler that was in the parking lot. The temperature on the lot was about 100 degrees so it was hotter than hell in the trailer. The teamsters let them out after a short time, and as they did one asked, "Hey, what are you guys doing in there? I bet no one told you about truck trailers in MBA school."

The guy sitting with me continued. "We come here every day knowing what our jobs are. It's simple. We move shit from one truck to another, from one side of the terminal to another. It's like watching the entire economy every day. I can see where the stuff is coming from and where it's going. Sometimes I go have daydreams about where everything ends up and wish I was there instead of here. But the daydreams end as soon as my supervisor gets in my face. Then I spend the rest of my shift trying to get back at the supervisor without him knowing it. The way I get back is to load the heavy shit on top of the other stuff in the trailer."

Management Style: Using Gridiron Greats

The teamster sitting with me went on to talk about the company's management style. "The Company hires management trainees right out of college, most of them former college football players. No doubt, the CEO believes it takes a football player to handle us. He should meet my wife! He thinks that these new trainees need to spend time out here with us blue-collar people if they're ever going to be a good manager. The problem is that they learn all the wrong things. What they learn is: don't trust the little people and make sure you always let people know who's the boss. It's like the guy beating the drum so the rowers on the Viking ships know what to do. So what these trainees do is boss us around and yell and curse at us, even though we've been doing this job for years while two months ago they were drinking beer at some fraternity house. They even say things like, 'You're not paid to think from the neck up. Just do your job.' So I say to myself, 'Fine. I'll move faster and load this shipment of river rocks on top of these stereo speakers. I'll never see this truck again anyway.'

"All the stuff gets broken for no good reason other than our revenge. It's only a matter of time before customers start going to other truck companies. When they do, and we start having layoffs and the union guys go crazy, I doubt the CEO will get hurt. He will probably get a big severance package. It will be us that have to cut back on our time or wages. It doesn't make sense. All the CEO has to do is spend ten minutes with us listening, get rid of the kid football player supervisors, and give us a little slice in deciding how things get done around here. I think the CEO is afraid to make any changes. I hope this guy (the CEO) burns in hell."

I can think of nothing worse than working with cowards or a cowardly leader. Worse, I fear cowardice might be contagious. And working with wimps will make one out of any of us, too. If cowardly leaders abound, it won't be long before the competition of stronger character will take over and there will be layoffs ... so start to look for a job now. Run to every job-hunting website that exists. Run.

Signs of a Cowardly CEO

- Poor Public Relations: Believes his own PR and hides behind a staff of handlers and promoters. Never jumps into the mosh pit of his own employees.

- Bad Attention Span: Is nicknamed "ADD Guy" because any time bad news comes up he immediately changes the subject to something more positive—usually about him. Will not confront bad news or tables it to the next meeting.

- Not Showing Up: Attendance is poor. He is never around when the big issues come up. "Works from home" even though he has so many homes no one knows where that is. Especially true in difficult times.

- Delegates Difficult Decisions: A cowardly leader will spend time deciding which band will play at the holiday party while decisions like staff reductions are left to others.

- Avoids Difficult Tasks: Always does the easiest tasks on his To Do List. Never gets to the hard ones. The hard ones never get off his list.

- Vindictiveness: When confronted, he gets even behind the scenes and then blames others for the misfortune. Acts like a bully behind the scenes and talks about others when they are not in the room. See the Nixon Tapes.

- Defensiveness: Always has excuses and never lets alternate points of view into the discussion.

- Roars: Reminds everyone of the Lion in the Wizard of OZ in the early parts of the movie. Might use the phrase, "I'll slit him from top to bottomus."

CEO After Dark

Jake was an 800 SAT score kind of CEO of a high tech company. The numbers and the analysis around the numbers made him feel alive. Dealing with the people side of the business, not so much. The thought of leading an "all hands meeting" or even doing a performance review made him break out in hives. The paradox was that he was smart enough to know about people's performance and about quality of their work; he just didn't want to deal with the people themselves.

Since he was on his computer most of the day, and not dealing with people, he decided that the best way to communicate was at night, when no one was in their cubicles. He would write messages on post-it notes and stick them on managers' computer screens while the janitors were cleaning up the office. Every morning the managers would dread looking at their computer screens and finding the yellow notes that said, "Make this report crisper" or "Project way behind— Fix it!" The messages were often ignored.

All the employees called it MYS (Management by Yellow Stickies) and thought the CEO was not brave enough to deal with the people.

 TEMPTATION

Temptations abound when it comes to courageous decisions and actions. There is always the hope that not showing the courage to deal with something will make it go away. Lunch could get in the way; another meeting might seem more important; and the tyranny of the calendar can reign supreme, often in the form of, "I can't deal with this now. I am too busy." But when we take off the blinders, pull away the pillows from our ears, and remove the covers we've pulled up to our nose, issues are still there—sometimes worse.

The lure of delegating big problems to others (like unsuspecting consultants) is strong, but delegation only sets up and reinforces the perception of the CEO as a coward. A rule that CEOs need to learn is that employees always know what is going on in the company. If there are acts of cowardice to behold, employees see them.

It is not unusual for a CEO to insulate himself from the day-to-day activities of the business. It is too easy to enjoy the trappings of the corner office and grow detached from the real work.

In the 2009 demise of General Motors, perhaps the most damning criticism of Rick Wagoner, the ousted CEO, was that he "lacked the courage" to change the organization to make it successful. The sin of cowardice can be contagious from the top down and spell doom for the organization. But there is hope. Corporate cowards will have plenty of company in hell.

 REDEMPTION

The vast majority of CEOs must demonstrate resolve all the time; they do not have the luxury of cowardice. But those few who are scaredy-cats can paint all the rest with the same brush. Lest I give the impression that all CEOs are cowards, let me identify some who were absolutely the reverse: Bill Gates turned Microsoft on a dime when he saw the Internet was the future. Richard Schulze turned Best Buy into a retail giant by staking out territory in technology that no one else saw. Steve Jobs has reinvented Apple more times than Madonna has reinvented her image. Ed Whitacre, former CEO of AT&T, built the world's largest telecom company without ever being called a coward. All of these men demonstrated no fear when they were CEOs.

There is no courage syrup or training course for the CEO that will inject his soul with bravery and eliminate any tendencies toward cowardice. A course in presentation skills or how to handle a public relations emergency is not an antidote—although some seem to think so. Others would say that for a CEO to demonstrate courage all he needs to do is treat people fairly, create a winning strategy, and flawlessly execute on the strategy. Others would call that Leadership 101.

The sin of cowardice is a flaw that will lead to a short tenure for a CEO if his board of directors has the courage to recognize the flaw. If the board sees it and still does nothing, the board will join the CEO in the sin bin and be well on their way to presiding over failure.

Takeaways

Often enough, we all succumb to fear in the workplace. To stay off that path to the ultra-hot zone full of people you know you won't like, a few pointers may help:

- Do the things that require the most courage yourself. Delegating tough decisions and tasks will lead to a label of wimp, or worse.

- Know others' jobs. It is not possible to know everyone's job, but at some point in all organizations the rubber meets the road at a predictable spot—usually near the customer. Dealing with the toughest customer is a surefire way to show courage. The popularity of the TV show *Undercover Boss* is premised on the belief that the big boss has the courage to get down and dirty with people doing real jobs.

- Be willing to sacrifice. Real courage is doing the right thing that may cost you your job. Always, always do the right thing.

2

THE SIN: FIDDLING

Rome Is Burning and We're Off-site

"I would rather get a root canal than go to another big waste-of-time meeting. Rome is burning and we are fiddling away our time in meetings." So said a customer service manager in an insurance company while she looked at the blinking lights of people on hold.

That smoldering sentiment pervades many organizations. Survey after survey points out how much we in the workforce dislike meetings, but they keep on being scheduled. There are many varieties of confabs that we schedule religiously in our high tech devices or in a leather bound "at-a-glance" book. The list includes the weekly staff meeting, the planning meeting, the budget meeting, the sales meeting, and the pipeline meeting. But many believe they all sort of have the same result—not much except keeping the local Starbucks and bagel shops in business.

How to Get Out of Work: Meetings

Meetings are the best way to get out of real work. When you are the CEO, you can call as many meetings as you want and get out of as much work as you can.

Spending too much time in meetings is like doing time in Limbo with other sinners. We can feel like we're in a state of suspended animation after a day of back-to-back-to-back PowerPoint discussions where everyone is trying to sneak looks at their Blackberries and iPhones. Meetings are not usually the way to increase revenue or productivity, enhance the culture, or do anything that the CEO is supposed to do. For the rest of us, the same holds true: meetings will probably not help us meet our personal or professional goals. We might enjoy some meetings because they allow us create a new To Do List or practice up on the video game Brick Breaker, but it is a rare meeting that is satisfying.

STERNO-WORLD MEETINGS: THE OFF-SITE

Of all the meeting types, worst of all might be the "off-site meeting." The off-site falls in a gray area of corporate life, somewhere between a vacation and work, but fulfills neither. Most people I know don't consider hanging around with co-workers, yellow stickies, and flip charts as a vacation, and getting any real work done at these events never really happens. Yet, the off-site continues unabated, a boon to the economy of every resort with large conference rooms and plenty of Sterno fuel for under the coffee and buffet trays.

The off-site meeting is a way to kill three weeks of work: a week to prepare, a week there, and a week to recover. Forget the lost time, the expense, and the goofy ice-breaking exercises (name your favorite animal); the meetings can be a way to build teams as everyone agrees they would rather be somewhere else. There are occasional cases, however, when more work gets done since leaders are all off-site and don't get in the way back at the ranch.

TEAM BUILDING WITH A SMILE

Frisbee, golf, scavenger hunts, good wine, an occasional swing from ropes, seeing co-workers do things they wouldn't ordinarily do—this is what I remember most of the best management retreats. At really bad ones, going through exercises like falling backwards (hoping people I don't know will catch me) or telling strangers "Ten Things You Don't Know About Me" are vivid memories. The CEO was always there leading the charge and always the first one to jump out of the tree or to swing from the rope. At some retreats during ropes exercises, attendees visualized how they wished the CEO was swinging from a different kind of rope.

Many consider the off-site meeting as a good way to do "research" about nice places to go back to when joined by one's spouse. That's all.

Called by many names, the Off –Site, the Planning Retreat, or the Strategic Planning Session is that special time when senior people in the organization go away to a nice place that the attendees cannot take advantage of while there. Invariably, those back at the organization that were not invited feel left out, but only because they have no idea they have been given a "get out of forced exile with your co-workers card." Except in those cases where more work actually gets done when the team is left alone, productivity tends to go down while management is gone and the CEO is not making decisions.

For the enterprising—if-morally-bankrupt sort—the off-site offers the perfect opportunity to witness the bad behavior of others and store the memory away until the time it can be used for discreet blackmail. Much of the early time at any off-site is focused on what is wrong with the organization. There is no organization that doesn't have a long list of things to be fixed, and the CEO, especially a new one, plans to fix them all. Ask President Obama.

The discussions usually focus on two unsolvable issues: one, communications; and two, how to get rid of the many-poor performing people that have been tolerated for lo these last many years. Neither issue is resolved at the end of most retreats, but someone dutifully records the sentiments about each on flip charts with a variety of colored markers. Yellow stickies may punctuate the doodles, words, and bullets that the recorder posts. The flip chart sheets are dutifully rolled up at the end of the meeting and will be propped vertically in the corner of someone's office, never to be read again.

Most retreats run out of time before solutions can be created, but everyone feels better once the general problems have been identified. At the end, the CEO thanks all for coming and explains how this is a watershed moment in the life of the organization.

The CEO has committed the fiddling sin. He has wasted two days fiddling away everyone's time. Nothing was done and nothing will change.

CEOs pay the bill for off-sites and often justify their participation in one of two ways. Some say, "I don't want to influence everyone so I want to be more of a participant and hear out everyone's opinion." Others say, "This is a chance for me to really demonstrate my take-charge leadership." It doesn't matter which way the CEO chooses to go, the meeting is "owned" by the CEO and he cannot get off that hook. If the meeting is not successful, if it fails to generate actual plans, it will be seen as a boondoggle and distraction from the real work of the business.

At best, the off-site might be appreciated for its entertainment value. And such seeming entertainment might make it all worthwhile. Although some are more effective than others, there can be entertainment value in almost all off-sites…

The Psychic and the Off-Site

Katina is a psychic, the kind you see with a blinking light out in front of her studio. We had retained her as spunky comic relief, a break, from the rigors of a retreat with a large group from a disc drive company. Katina is under thirty, good-looking, and can gaze into people's eyes and predict their future in a charming and engaging way. When we called to book her for the retreat it was half as a joke to do some entertaining after the first night's dinner. When we called she said, "I knew you would be calling." We knew immediately we were on to something.

After a childhood sickness, Katina lost 80 percent of her hearing. She would look at people's mouths as they spoke to try to understand what they were saying, but she also started to look into their eyes. Alarmingly accurate insights came to her as she would peer into the eyes of the talker. She found she could look deeply into the unsuspecting person's soul and see his or her future. It was truly believable and easy to understand how she could build a career around this gift. This was not a technique they had trained us in during graduate school.

Katina was on the retreat agenda as a unnamed "surprise session." The day had been filled with ten or twelve PowerPoint presentations with lots of spreadsheets and rehashing of the past. Katina was the after-dinner entertainment and was introduced with little fanfare, but the group was curious. It was the most interesting part of the day. She explained her hearing loss story and made some predictions for the company and the people in it—all good. Then she announced that if anyone would like an individual session, she was available. All fifty of the retreat participants lined up, including the CEO of this Fortune 500 Company, the leader of the off-site and, in fact, an industry luminary. It was funny at first, but then I realized that the retreat was quickly unraveling. Why bother going through the rigor of analytics and forecasting when Katina could do it more quickly (and credibly) than my world-class consulting team or the strategic planning group?

Needless to say, the remainder of the retreat involved only discussions about how to implement Katina's recommendations, which the CEO had written down. The company actually did follow Katina's advice. Although her advice often reiterated the obvious, like "Pay attention to your largest customers" and "You will attract an important new talent to the company. Make sure you welcome him," some would argue the counsel might have been just as good as anything that the MBAs could develop.

The Arc of the Off-Site

As one who has attended way too many long-range planning meetings, I have discovered the arc of those meetings goes something like this …

Optimism phase: Arrival through the morning of the first day. The entire team, all attendees, believe they are winners and that a clear plan for the future will emerge from a PowerPoint presentation by noon. The CEO says so. You will hear themes like "The Future is Here" and "Unsurpassed Performance" and "Global Leader" and the unlimited size of the market. The afternoon will be for golf and spas, and everyone will be jumping out of their skin with anticipation. The facilitator makes each person introduce him- or herself and share expectations with the rest of the group. She has handfuls of yellow stickies. The expectations always include the phrases "clear direction" and "roadmap." The expectations for the CEO are sky high. He is smiling and clapping his hands. Alright, let's get to it!

Uh-oh. There seems to be some confusion between "a vision" and "a mission." Many flip chart pages later, we are close to having a set of statements that everyone agrees to but no one cares about any longer. The hanging point seems to be should the central phrase be "global leader" or "number one in the market"? At least three people are hiding a Blackberry as they play with it on their lap.

The CEO has canceled golf and spas because setting the context for the future is just too darn important. A grey cloud is slowly forming on the horizon of the windowless room.

12:00 lunch of the first day: A welcome break. You join people whose names you have heard but you don't know. All of you discuss your hopes for more free time at the next meeting, and wouldn't it be great to be like one of the people you can see out of the windows? The CEO casually joins a table; he is one of the "people."

Ambition phase: Afternoon of the first day. You suspect a complete detailed plan for the future may not emerge today, but still hope for it by the end of the retreat. How could the CEO leave without a plan? In the back of your mind you are starting to think you will settle for a road map on what you are supposed to do next month—you are willing to call it a To Do list. You want to focus, commit to work with full concentration all afternoon for completion, but the facilitator is moving way too slowly and smiling too much. She is flicking the pads of colored stickies like playing cards. All wives of attendees are out shopping in the expensive boutiques nearby, probably feeling alone and irritated. All husbands of attendees are home with the kids. You are calculating how much the shopping trip, or your absence from home, may cost you.

By the end of the afternoon there are hundreds of flip chart pages around the walls. There could be thousands of stickies spread around. Even if readable, most of the writing is gibberish, with words and phrases like "quality," "performance," "focus," and "what can we stop doing?" sprinkled in different colors. The only good news is you are starting to think the facilitator is high from the fumes of the markers and may start singing a Fleetwood Mac song. The question is asked about whether or not we should change the agenda to start earlier tomorrow. No one thinks that should happen except the CEO, but there is a long debate anyway. You decide to start at the appointed time so as not to screw up the hotel catering. The CEO is overruled by catering. Your ambition for the meeting is starting to wilt, and everyone in the room is thinking, "Where is the bar?"

6:00 pm of the first day: Everyone drinks heavily and eats too much at the buffet. You look around to join and meet people you don't know, but sit next to all the people you know anyway. A Jimmy Buffet impersonator is the entertainment after dinner, and the CEO is dancing with his assistant.

The hotel bar is packed at midnight with retreat attendees. Everyone is feeling proud to be a part of this organization.

Realism phase: Morning of the second day. You are assigned to breakout groups and spend all morning talking about company problems instead of your assigned task. In the final ten minutes, you assign an unwilling recorder and presenter and tackle the assigned problem. The solution you develop has been tried before and failed. Doubts about completing anything during the off-site start to creep in. People begin to worry if they will have to lay off some of their people when they return to the office. Each group makes a presentation and the CEO takes notes.

12:00 lunch of the second day: The escape fantasy is tested. People are wondering if attendance will be taken at the afternoon meetings. Using what creative juices remain, people may plan an elaborate scheme to escape, but chicken out at the last minute. The CEO doesn't join lunch; he is in the hall on his cell phone.

Promissory phase: Afternoon, the second day. As everyone returns to the meeting room, the CEO proclaims that much work needs to be done off-line. This takes all afternoon. Consulting firms may be brought in for help so that a "new direction" will emerge, and there is consensus that this may be money well spent. Everyone agrees consultants are a good idea and bolts for the door. People begin to worry about their own job.

Evening of the second day: More heavy drinking than the first night. Attendees compare websites for job hunting. The CEO and his assistant aren't there.

Completion phase: Morning of the third day. An expensive speaker is there—a former CEO of a company who received a huge exit package. Although her message is good, everyone is trying to figure out how to get a similar payout and why she is so lucky. The CEO and the speaker are good friends. Everyone shakes hands, says good-byes until next year, and gets back to work. The meeting planners are wildly thanked in the final speech and evaluations are distributed. The meeting is proclaimed a big success by the CEO.

We have all been to this meeting, probably more than once. The CEO who sponsors these meetings is a sinner. If you helped put this meeting together and let it happen, you are complicit in the sin. This meeting was a waste of time, and worse, no one was allowed to have a good time as a reward for just being there.

TEMPTATION

There is a real lure to any retreat: time away from the office commotion and the phone and the email to really think about the business. What a concept! Yet, phone and email follow us, in our pocket in the form of some mobile device. We are all always connected, and it is easier to accept that Facebook invitation via Blackberry than it is to think hard about the business. If that is what you are going to do, stay home and save everyone a lot of money.

The temptation in this case—to eliminate distractions in order to clarify big ideas and strategic thinking—is a good concept. The reality of wasting time and money without producing a real outcome is where the sin of fiddling is committed. Fiddling or wasting time while the most important things are just not getting done will soon lead to malaise, which will lead to even worse outcomes.

The recent financial meltdown had major banks holding off-site planning sessions in Boca Raton and the Bahamas. They were all New York-based banks.

A California-based financial services firm held their annual long-range planning retreat at an exclusive ski resort. It was both difficult and expensive to get to the resort. Because the business at hand was so critical, the bulk of the day was reserved for "hard core" planning, and the attendees were instructed they could ski between 7 and 9 am or after 5 pm. The ski lifts opened at 9 and closed at 5. The attendees were so grouchy the entire time that nothing was accomplished. That CEO was fiddling and torturing at the same time.

It is tempting to fiddle—we all do it—but it doesn't get anyone off our backs or get the project done. The temptation to fiddle happens every day, all day; it is just that the off-site is the perfect vehicle for fiddling at the highest levels. The off-site retreat has an arc to it, like a play or a movie, each phase full of temptations.

Contrary to popular belief, retreats are really hard work for all who attend. Foremost, there's nowhere to hide. Anyone who monopolizes the airtime is assumed to be jockeying for a promotion. Anyone who doesn't participate is assumed to have checked out. Yet, the CEO often doesn't see it.

 REDEMPTION

Off-site meetings can be helpful. There are plenty of guides on how to run a meeting. Here are just a few unorthodox tips from the perspective of a sympathetic veteran of off-sites:

- If the CEO is in the room, it is his meeting. Even if he is there to observe, he is the one who will make the decisions and is evaluating what is happening in the meeting. Don't confuse his passive attendance with his ceding power to others.

- At an off-site, assuming you are in a desirable place, embrace it. Don't close the windows. Why go to Hawaii if there is no time for the pool or golf, and people are locked in dark rooms from 8 AM to 8 PM? In a resort, the more free time the better the meeting will be. I have never heard of an off-site being held in Hamburg or Newark.

- Teach. Don't try to do real work. People want to learn at meetings, even if that means how to construct an effective plan or understand market dynamics. Stress will be the order of the day if there is neither teaching nor planning happening. Bring in speakers who can teach and entertain at the same time and keep the meeting short. If it's all real work, stay home and just do real work.

- Never put lawyers as the first speakers on the agenda. Sarbanes Oxley compliance is not new, and not uplifting.

- Never start with a blank piece of paper: If you need to do a vision and mission, draft one beforehand. It will be 90 percent right and no one will pay attention to the other 10 percent. There are mission/vision formulators on the web.

- Invite someone who will dance in the evenings. The success of the entertainment depends on someone getting up there early in the evening to pretend they are on *Dancing with the Stars*. Pay someone to dance if you have to.

- Entertainment will never please everyone. If you had the Beatles as the entertainers, people would complain. Get over it.

- Spread out the chairs. I like my space and, if I have to sit too close to people in chairs that are connected to each other, I go to the dark side—probably better described as poolside.

- Check cell-phones at the door. At most PGA events today, all devices that can ring, ping, or otherwise receive or send messages must be checked at the gate. An unenforceable rule for meetings, but wouldn't it be nice? An alternative is to have everyone tape their thumb to their index finger upon registration.

- Present a realistic agenda. Too many meetings include way too many items with wildly unrealistic timeframes: "In the morning we will solve world hunger, and after lunch we will fix the peace process in the Middle East." It should be more like: "Tell me what the agenda is and I will participate wholeheartedly, but make it a good agenda and stick to it when I get there."

- Death by PowerPoint is a real terminal activity. A surefire way to kill a meeting? Line up PPT presentations from 8 AM through 4 PM. Alternatives to PPT include discussions and meaningful exchanges.

- People will drink too much—it's an automatic. You are not responsible for anyone's drunken behavior. Put a sign over each bar that says: Drink Heavily—Remember You Are Young, Marketable, and Willing to Relocate.

- *Tchotchkes* (a Yiddish word for trinket or souvenir) are so of the last economy. If you are thinking of cheap giveaways like key chains and Frisbees, don't do it. People will see that expense and think it will cost them next year's bonus.

- Beware of dermatologists. I went to a corporate meeting at the same resort that was concurrently hosting a dermatologist convention. No one would go to the pool or play golf without guilt.

- Tell attendees to bring their family at their own risk. I once flew across the country to Disney World with young children on my lap. Once we got there, they erased my presentation from my computer and only wanted to play with the buttons in the elevator, not go into the park. Everyone's expectations of special family time at corporate meetings are way off—in the wrong direction.

- Remember that anything and everything you do at a meeting could, and will, show up on YouTube.

The most important outcome, if not the only thing to come out of an off-site meeting, is the creation of a tone for the entire organization. All meetings set the tone of the organization, but especially big meetings like the "off-site." A common sense approach to these seminal meetings may keep any CEO out of hell. A simple example is the paradox of expense cuts raging throughout the organization, with an off-site in a luxurious resort. Talk about leadership not exercising any commonsense judgment. Forget the deposit already placed on the hotel. No one believes you can't break the contract and no one will remember deposits. But everyone will remember the Ritz Carlton meetings during layoffs.

Takeaways

Our lives are full of meetings. You are in them, you call them, and you lead them. There are big ones that are off-site, and smaller, less grand ones that fill every day. If meetings are poorly conceived and sloppy, other parts and processes of the organization will follow. If there is no specific goal for an outcome or agenda, the organization will wander through the desert of no goals. If meetings are a waste of time, kill them. If meetings are essential, make them effective. We all know which ones can be eliminated and which ones are critical to the success of the organization.

Meetings tend to be managed well in any billable time environment, like law firms or consulting firms. Every internal meeting takes away from time that can be billed. Although not necessarily the model, the simple question "How much is this meeting costing us?" can change behavior in and around meetings.

Every locker room has inspirational sayings that gather no attention hanging on the walls. But there is almost always one focused question that defines what happens on the practice field and in meetings. At Michigan it might be, "What have you done today to beat Ohio State?" At UCLA, it might be "What have you done today to beat USC?" and so on. In the front of every meeting room there could be that same one focused question that asks, "What will this meeting do to make our organization more successful?" That might be all it takes to cancel some meetings and build that better mousetrap.

A poor leader will sponsor a meeting where everyone has the sense of fiddling while more important things need to be done. A real leader will kill the fiddlers and host meetings that are thresholds through which progress is made. Fiddlers will fall off the roof.

3

THE SIN: WAFFLING

It's Never "Whatever"

The chairs were arranged in the conference room for a high drama meeting between the consultants and the client, a Fortune 500 company. The attendees chose seats carefully, recognizing there was an unwritten protocol of who sat where. George, the CEO, sat prominently at the head of the table. I was the lead consultant on this ever so stressful project, and it was a tricky situation involving the potential elimination of thousands of jobs. The projector was humming, ready for my PowerPoint presentation. The junior consultants were seated in a circle at the wall, away from the table, not ready for the "grown-up" table yet. Only one consultant and the ranking VPs from the company were allowed at the long, shiny conference table, each with a full water bottle at his place. This was not a time for business casual, either literally or figuratively. It was a time for tense decision making about people's lives.

Lives in the Balance

The lives in question were women's. Large operator centers are staffed mostly with women. Picture low-slung buildings with no windows, each building filled with small cubes, each cube full of *tchotchkes* and family photos and occupied by a woman wearing a headset. Lots of these women were about to lose their jobs.

The meeting was the end result of a long project to determine where this major telecom company was going to locate the operator centers after consolidation. Consolidation is another way to spell layoffs. There had been a megamerger, and now there were just way too many of everything—people, equipment, facilities, and locations. The consulting project considered how and where to consolidate and reduce the number of centers. Instead of twenty locations, there would now be only three; seventeen cities would be scrambling and screaming, trying to save jobs. It is a scene that has been played out hundreds of times recently.

People with PhDs in operations research were involved. Focus groups had been conducted. The slicing and dicing of the data was extensive and included what the consultants joked was "double inverted activity analysis." Everyone wanted to do this right because at least 6,000 people were about to lose their jobs, and it would be all over the national headlines.

The presentation was crisp and the case was made for the changes we proposed, even though they were a foregone conclusion. But no one really paid attention to the data or the platitudes about how the communications industry was changing. Everybody was waiting for the "answer." Each slide provided a clue as to where the new centers could be located. But by the time the final slide was presented, no one in the room, except me and the other consultants, knew the cities that would be listed on the recommendation page—the last page of fifty.

The final slide was the denouement, when it would all came together and the choices would be clear. As I was about to click onto that page, I tried to break the tension by saying, "I know this is the page you've been waiting for. Are you sure you want me to show it?" The joke was not well received, so I clicked forward.

PICK A CITY, ANY CITY

On the slide were the names of five cities. Our task had been to narrow it down to five, and the company would pick three based on our criteria and what the CEO knew about all the company issues. Everyone saw the cities, and I was sure there were no surprises. It was time for the "facilitated discussion," so I encouraged the CEO, with the help of other execs in the room, to pick the three cities out of the five named on the slide. The work had been done. It was now decision time and that was now the CEO's job.

He looked at the slide, puckered his mouth, and virtually spit out the word "Whatever!"

There was a stunned silence, especially from me since I was up front. I was thinking WTF, but I thought he might be attempting to make a joke. Everyone continued to look at the slide until finally I said, "'Whatever' is not one of the cities on the page." With that, George got up and walked out of the room with his entourage in tow. As they were leaving, I said to no one in particular, "Wait! What the hell does "whatever" mean?" I felt like I was dealing with dignitaries from North Korea over nuclear testing.

How could this be? Lives hung in the balance. City economies were involved. The CEO had committed the huge sin of waffling with a capital W. By not making this critical decision the consequences were staggering and sinful.

When he said "Whatever!" what he really meant was, "You make the decision, Mr. Wise Ass-Consultant, so that I can blame you for all the problems that will surely ensue."

Eventually, the decision was made. I would like to say that the final verdict came after a lot of imposed deadlines by the consultants. Instead, word of the changes leaked to the newspaper, a decision was made, and thousands of women did lose their jobs. One CEO who liked the word "whatever" never quite regained his career trajectory and turned into a bigger nexus of indecision. He was a waffler and a sinner.

 TEMPTATION

The most egregious sin that a leader can commit is the sin of indecision, the sin of waffling. CEOs are paid to make decisions, but so are middle managers and anyone else who shows up to do a job. Just about everyone in any organization is paid to make decisions. When a leader at the US Postal Service a few years ago proclaimed that, "Our people are not paid to think from the neck up," there was a firestorm of controversy. We all make decisions, all day every day.

Wafflers defer decisions and sometimes don't make them at all. Any waffling—that which exploits the word "whatever" or that which appears through ambivalent actions—will mean less action, less forward movement, less direction, and less job security. Shrugging shoulders, not returning messages, not showing up, not expressing thoughts clearly, and revisiting every decision are other symptoms of the waffler. It is often easier to waffle than it is to make a decision, even a small one. We are all probably guilty of the waffle sin from time to time.

What do you do when the "CHECK ENGINE" light starts flashing on your car dashboard while you're driving along? Do you make the decision to make an appointment for service; do you pull over to see if you are leaking oil? If you're like me, you keep driving and hope the light will turn off. Decisions don't usually go away. Our temptation to believe they will leads to the sin of waffling.

The Abusive Waffler

Sean, the CEO of a software company in San Francisco, was known to be mercurial. He was the founder of the company as well, and everyone cut him some slack for being a "genius." A typical day included him throwing soda cans and chairs at employees. As you might imagine, he terrified the people around him. His bouts were often induced by someone making a decision that he didn't like— and his retracting the decision. The problem was, once he took the decision back, he would hold on to it and review it over and over but never make any further decision. He would waffle. People in the organization criticized his lack of decision making just as much as his abusive behavior. In fact, they believed the guilt induced by his being a constant waffler is what made him abusive.

Waffling is a trait we despise in our leaders; just ask any politician who can't shake the label of flip-flopper. A leader's failure to make decisions, no matter how big or small, is obvious to employees, customers and investors, and does not inspire confidence.

A KEY WAFFLE INDICATOR—ONE WORD: "WHATEVER"

Waffling is easy; we could play out the "whatever" waffle sin every day. While a certain amount of idling is necessary for even the most productive people, indulging in pastimes rather than tackling what is most important is a subtle way of declaring "whatever." Consider that next time you show up and drain email, or check Facebook instead of making a customer call. What's "around," what's fun, what's cool, what's in front of you is often not what needs to be done.

Waffling kills all the confidence others have in you to get them to the organizational "promised land." Imagine being on an airplane, listening to channel nine on a flight home. You know the channel: the one full of static, where the pilot and air traffic control are chirping back and forth about turns and checkpoints and runways and weather and traffic. You know your own flight number so you can track what your pilot is saying to air traffic control. After a directive from ATC, your airplane pilot responds: "Whatever!" Time to reach for the airsickness bag.

The CEO who sends off the whatever message in any form seems to be saying that he doesn't care. But it could be that he really does, and if he knew the signal that "whatever" is sending he would change. The one who doesn't care or change is surely the sinner.

At one time when I heard the word "whatever," it had only one meaning: "I don't give a shit." Or, as my friends in the teamsters union would say when they heard "whatever," the "give a shit factor" was so low it didn't matter. As in, "They both have to wait for their marriages to be annulled before they can get married. Whatever." Now I know that the word, when used by a leader, is full of nuance and complicated meanings, none of them heartening, all leading to sins.

When a CEO utters, mumbles, or declares "whatever," or any relative of the word, he really means something from the list below:

THE TOP EIGHT DEFINITIONS OF "WHATEVER"

1. I don't care.
The act of sorting through priorities is a critical activity of anyone's day, or life for that matter. When faced with making decisions, the response of "whatever" means "I don't care. The outcomes are all the same." The belief that the outcomes "are the same and don't matter" is rarely true.

2. You make the decision for me. I will blame you later.
Often used in response to a question when the CEO doesn't want to make a decision. Another frequent usage is between two people who are fighting but won't admit it. This is a passive-aggressive response where no one does what they really want to do.

3. If I knew the answer, I would tell you. So leave me alone.
This is sort of a guessing game where "whatevers" can be exchanged back and forth. Like, "What do you want to do? … I don't know. What do you want to do?" A vicious circle is created where no one will make a decision, but since the CEO is involved, he wins.

4. I am not listening.
A common emanation from CEOs, which means the decision is not important enough for him to make. Then, who will make it?

5. **Of all the options presented, none are good. But I know you need my input, so I will make you suffer with my ambivalence.**
A form of paralysis in an organization when the CEO instructs the troops. No one knows what to do so everyone guesses.

6. **I am quite pissed off and, regardless of my decision, I will hold you responsible for it.**
If "whatever" is uttered with a sigh and a chilly tone, the CEO is probably being forced into making a decision that he never wanted to make. Just the thought of the consequences of either decision has him liking you less by the second. It's time to put a resume together.

7. **I don't have an opinion, so I will fill the air with this useless word.**
There is always white space in the conversation that can be filled up with words, especially by a CEO. "Whatever" is often used an effective filler with the added subtle meaning of "I don't care."

8. **Even though I am the CEO, I am resigned to being a victim of life and the world.**
This usage of "whatever" may be the most common and the most devastating for all involved. It can be heard in phrases like "I am trapped" or "I am stuck" or "What's the use?" said with one deep breath and a sigh. The only response I can think of is, "Hey, if you don't want to be a CEO, then quit! And for the rest of us, If we experience such a sense of futility that our approach to work and life is governed by a dismal "whatever," then it's time for big changes.

Survey Says: Whatever!

A poll was conducted by researchers at Marist College in Poughkeepsie, New York. The simple question was: "What is the most annoying phrase or word for 2010?"

The winner was the word *whatever.*

Some 39 percent of those polled ranked *whatever* as the nation's most annoying word, far surpassing the second-most hated word "*like,*" which rankled just 28 percent of respondents in the random telephone survey of more than 1,000 individuals. *Whatever* was also the most annoying word of 2009.

It's worth mentioning that the survey, which broke down statistics based on age, income, gender, and several other demographic slices (such as whether you have kids in your household), found that *whatever* annoyed nearly universally, though you were somewhat more likely to find the word annoying if you were 45 or older, white, and didn't have kids in your household.

A SMALL DECISION IS STILL A DECISION

Choices, decisions, and options—they happen over and over all day, every day. There is an occasional big one that comes along, like "Should I hire that new CIO who will want to spend a lot of money?" But most are small choices. Still, no decision is too small for our consideration. Seemingly small decisions are often the ones that make a big difference. Deferring or avoiding a decision, however minor it may seem, could carry consequences and make for a life of coulda's, woulda's, shoulda's.

Small decisions are like empty airline seats: once the plane takes off, it's too late for the airline to worry about filling the seat. If that small decision is not made, it is quickly too late to worry about what could have been. Any decision, big or small, that is not made is another step into hell.

It is clear to me that a successful CEO is one who has learned to make decisions. It's taken for granted that the big choices are worth the attention they receive. We agonize over them, analyze them, consult with gurus over them, chart them, and—admit it— we all make lists of pros and cons about those big choices. And we should. The everyday, seemingly little choices deserve a little space in the brain, too, and should not be relegated to the "whatever" dumper.

Our natural tendency is to defer choices whenever we can, like my client who proclaimed "whatever" when it came to the operator centers with thousands of job losses in the balance.

When my kids were little, I would give them a choice at bedtime: you can either go to bed, or you can take a bath and go to bed. That set of choices didn't last long because soon they chose neither. The choices are usually not so clear in the workplace for the CEO.

REORGS R Us

No matter the issue, Mark knew the answer. And the answer was: "REORG". If the plant burnt down, reorg. If someone resigns, reorg. If marketing can't get along with engineering, reorg. Someone submitted a suggestion that the company change its name to Reorg Inc. The problem was that a corporate reorganization was not necessarily the answer to the problem. What every reorg did was create a tremendous amount of activity but not necessarily move the company toward meeting its goals. Nonetheless, with lots of steering committees and meetings, all chaired by Mark, he could preside over the constant fiddling while the company went no where. He was sinning and fiddling and eating coffee and doughnuts all at once.

 REDEMPTION

Closure is King

People like college because every term has a beginning, middle, and an end. Along the way, we choose just how hard we want to work in every class, consciously or not, and live with the results.

People like to work out because they can make a choice about how many sets to do of a given exercise and complete an activity based on that choice. In our work lives, such sense of completion is rare. In fact, most jobs are designed so that they are never done, never complete. No wonder closure and accomplishment are so elusive and the "whatever" attitude can prevail.

The CEO who waffles and burbles "whatever, whatever, whatever" is a major sinner because of his indecision and the paralysis that ensues. In your career, in your dealings with others, and in all daily challenges, there's no better alternative than making a choice and living with it. Don't avoid, defer, or pass the buck to someone else. "The buck stops here," with you, and the bucks sure will stop accruing if no one makes decisions. Make choices based on your intuition and knowledge, worry as you need to, and move on.

Safra was one of the best CEOs I ever saw in action because she was a decision maker. It was that simple. It was typical for her to announce to her assembled executive team, "I have heard everyone who I think can weigh in on this matter and here is what we are going to do…" The team would listen, and whether they agreed or not, she would lay out the course of action and that was what they did. She would also say corny things like, "If there is no wind, row," but she never said "whatever." Her belief was that moving forward with a semirational decision was better than standing still. If the movement was not forward, at least there was movement—and it was rarely backwards. And if it was backwards, Safra would find lessons and opportunities to change course. She was not destined for hell. In fact, Safra is destined for a career full of respect and remuneration because she can make a decision.

The lesson is simple: A well-informed decision, regardless of the outcome, is better than no decision or ambivalence or … whatever.

GIVE US THIS DAY OUR DAILY CHOICE

Decisions, decisions, decisions. Sometimes, when they least want to make a decision, even a small one, CEOs are forced into choosing. Times like every day when you wake up and have to decide what to wear and how to approach the day. Times like when you have had a really bad day and your sixteen-year-old asks to extend his curfew so that he can stay out later. Times like when your boss asks you to do something extra, and you really don't want to do it.

Your approach and the choices you make in each of these situations are important. How you appear to others, and the attitude with which you approach the day could tell the world that you are worth spending time with or that you don't care. How you deal with the curfew extension could be one small part of a complex relationship with a teenager. Your answer to your boss could signal, "I am part of the team" or "Take this job and shove it," as in, "OK, I will do it (but I don't want to and will get even with you eventually)."

No one is saying choices will be easy, even the small ones. When you choose to stay up too late talking to your daughter about her new boyfriend, you can be sure that someone will be waiting for you at work first thing in the morning to discuss why your project is behind schedule, overstaffed, and in need of some major decisions at the next steering committee.

Choices, decisions, options—they happen over and over all day, every day, 24/7. There is an occasional big one that will come your way, like, "Should I take that new job in another city?" But most are small choices. The small ones are easy to gloss over, but it is those small choices that make the difference. The small ones are often the choices that we make everyday that impact our health, our relationships, our career.

I have called out the word "whatever" as a symptom of indecision, but the "whatever" word could easily be replaced by a shrug, no answer, a raise of the eyebrows, or a kick of the dog when you get home.

To be clear, there is a set of "Big Decisions." These are the decisions that change the trajectory of a life or a relationship. These are the decisions that make for the high drama in Hollywood. These are the decisions that we look back on with awe and wonder, or with "what was I thinking at the time?" Here are some of the big ones:

- Marriage/Relationships: Is he/she the one, or can I do better if I wait? How will I know? Is this the last chance? What if I make a mistake?

- Children: Do I want them? When? How many? What if I can't have any? What if I don't want any—will anyone marry me?

- Geography: Not only what area, but once in that area, will it be the suburbs or the country or the city? An apartment, a house, or the back of a VW bus?

- Career: What if I don't know what to do? Should I do what I like or what will allow me to get a job? How much money is realistic? Will I make a contribution to the greater good?

- Religion: Where do I start? What are my beliefs? What happens when I die? What if I don't like the religion in which I was raised?

- Lifestyle: There are risks and should I go after them? How ambitious do I want to be? Do I want a "Big Life" or a controlled life?

- For consideration: Tattoos and body piercings are not easy to change. Should I get fat? Should I have a face-lift? Should I save for retirement? Should I spend my life savings on a car?

The big decisions are like parallel universes that follow you through life. They never go away and you may struggle with careers, relationships, and geographies, or all of them, for your entire life. With some of them you will be second-guessing yourself forever. (What would have happened if Rhonda from high school hadn't dumped me?) The big ones never go away but are affected by all the daily smaller decisions we make.

Daily decisions might seem tedious and mundane, but they are the ones that make a difference. Ignoring them can send you to hell. They include:

- What to wear. When it enters your mind to say, *no one will notice*, they do.

- Whether or not to participate in a meeting. If you go, participate, or why bother?

- Make a new friend or have lunch with an old friend. Either way is good. Go out to lunch with friends.

- Listen and learn new things in that required training session.

- Wait for an upgrade or get one now.

- Should I miss the meeting and go to the soccer game?

- Should I get stuck in traffic or work from home?

- Should I do ten things at once and move them all forward a little bit, or pick one and finish it?

- Hit the mute button on a conference call and do other things, or participate?

Too often, like turning over the Magic Eight Ball, we see that the answer is hazy, so we moan and whine in that uncertainty. Work the small decisions because they are the ones that make the difference.

There are also big ones that we make which seem small, but can stay with us forever because we didn't know they were big at the time. Not paying attention in that sophomore accounting class could come back to haunt us. The choice made then can hurt later, and there might be a lot of those "choices." When someone tells you, "Someday you will pay for that," they are usually right.

There are millions of choices on the job, whether you are a CEO or clerk. Most of us choose to do the easy tasks while the challenging or onerous ones that are most critical to the organization or our career go unopened. The daily choice of how you spend your time is the biggest and most important variable of the day. Real work needs to get done.

The uncertainty that governs our world doesn't make choices easier. Uncertainty seems to gather around every decision we make—there are so many variables that affect them. As the number of choices increases, so does the potential for not making them. But the heaps and volumes of small decisions are what every one of us needs to make in the best way.

The Secret to a Marriage

Liz and Charles were celebrating their sixtieth wedding anniversary at a gala gathering of friends and family. Liz stood up, radiant, thanked all who were there, and spoke lovingly of her family and especially her husband, Charles. She was dressed elegantly, like it was the important occasion that it was, and she said with a clear voice, "It was love at first sight with Charles, and I love him more now than I did sixty years ago." Everyone was touched and through teary eyes knew that Charles was the winner in this deal.

When it was Charles's turn, he gathered the audience into his arms like he was teaching a class at the community college. He looked the role, too, in a frumpy blazer and baggy pants. With a smile in his voice he said, "I know what you all want to ask me. You want to ask, 'What is the secret to our long marriage?' Well, I am about to tell you. When we were first married, Liz and I had a meeting and we decided that I would make all the big decisions and she would make all the small decisions. I am here to tell you, after sixty years of marriage, I am still waiting for a decision to come my way."

Takeaways

We learn early that making a decision can establish the leader in a group. Visualize that group of young friends standing around with you when someone says, "What do you want to do?" followed by, "I don't know. What do you want to do?" and on and on. You know you have been there. Now remember the person who finally declared, "Let's go to the mall," and everyone trudged over to hang out at the mall. Maybe no one really wanted to go to the mall, but someone made a decision and maybe it wasn't a half-bad idea. Ambivalence never wins the day and is a sin no matter what your job level or what decision is before you.

It is way too easy to get trapped in the decision-making process and commit the sin of waffling or ambivalence. Even if you are not the CEO, ambivalence will doom you to a life of grey days and living in the white space of the organization chart ... and, possibly, to hell. For you to stay out of hell and be successful, there are some simple guidelines to follow, whether you are a CEO or "just someone trying to get by ..."

- Use the word "whatever" only when referring to commitments, not decisions, as in, "I will make this project successful, whatever it takes." In fact, make it easier; just **don't ever use the word "whatever."**

- Consider all options when making any decision, then **narrow them down to three** and pick one. There are hardly ever more than three options. Regarding careers, we are all asked the question, "What do you want to do?" I have always hated that question, but indecision eliminates choices. Try becoming a Navy pilot if you don't make the decision until you turn thirty-five years old.

- Use *Consumer Reports*-type charts, listing variables and options, when making big decisions. Those darkened or empty circles can change perspectives. Even after all the analysis, you still may have to **make a decision based on your experience and intuition.** And in those cases, just make one.

- Not all decisions are rational. **Listen to your emotions, too.** When buying our first house, my wife and I listed all the pros and cons of a particular house. There were fifty things listed on the cons' list and only a few listed on the pros' list. One of them was the wallpaper in the kitchen. We bought the house and loved it.

- Not all decisions are big ones, but even **small decisions should be addressed** because the small ones can get you closer to your goals and closest to what you might want. As in, "What do you want for lunch, the salad or the Rocky Mountain oysters?" When the small decisions pile up, they can become the big decisions that you need to make.

- **Make decisions and move on.** Second-guessing is never productive, and 20/20 hindsight is a pipedream. Just make those decisions based on clear thinking, experience, and information.

Remember Safra's simple words: "I've listened to what everyone had to say, taken all of your ideas into consideration, and I've decided this is what we are going to do." That's all it took for the organization to follow her faithfully without waffling.

Making objective, thoughtful decisions is a skill that's crucial to a successful career and life, no matter your rank or industry. The path to hell is paved with decisions that never saw the light of day … and an organization—or a life—full of coulda, woulda, shoulda.

4

THE SIN: PARALYSIS

Bald Tires and Building Coffins

An organization that is not growing and moving forward is dying. It is up to the CEO and all leaders to move the organization forward. Sounds simple, but the big reason organizations and their leaders often fail is inertia. And nothing creates inertia and discontent like too many priorities and lack of focus from the top. The sin that results and takes over is paralysis.

Snowstorms cause paralysis, but the snow melts and activity soon picks up again. The "system is down" causes paralysis, but it always comes back "up" and the screens light up with productivity quickly. Big events, both good and bad, like World Series victory parades or a local crisis can cause paralysis, but the parade is soon over and the meetings resume. When a leader causes paralysis, it can stick until he is gone.

Missions and strategies are fine, but nothing sets a direction like actions by the leader. The old saw of "actions follow intent" shows what's important and is based on what decisions are to be made. Where there is no set of actions and a lack of clear intent, nothing happens except sins. Lack of commonsense activities and lack of clear decisions engender inertia at all levels of a company. When leaders fail to recognize paralysis, more inactivity sets in and the big sin is compounded.

Paralysis doesn't mean that people aren't working. Often, even in a paralyzed environment, people are working their butts off. But one frustration borne of paralysis breeds even more contempt and sins. Nothing makes people more aggravated than a sense that they are working their butts off to no end, for no purpose. The person who defines that "end" and that "purpose" is the CEO. Without belief that there is a reason for the hard work, a sense of futility will prevail as well as a sense that the CEO doesn't know what the hell he is doing.

Action vs. Paralysis: Clarity Counts

The objective can be simple yet ambitious, as long as it tells a story: "We want to make more potato chips. We want to deliver pizzas faster than anyone else. We want to build a faster chip. We want to create drugs that will cure cancer. We want to build an affordable electric car. We want to save the land in Sonoma County."

These are goals that create a platform and make everyone feel that they can add a plank. Inaction happens when goals are not clear, and that is a sin committed by leaders at all levels of any organization. As a software developer told me, "It is difficult to act on the goal of providing value justification in a just-in-time environment."

The Devil You Know

At one all-hands meeting of a large bank, the CEO, who was approached with the accusation that no one knew where the company was going, retorted, "Do you think we don't have a strategy, or do you think we are not telling anyone?"

I jumped out of my skin with another question that I didn't ask out loud: "Which is worse?" And does it matter?

ROTATING BALD TIRES

Depending on the organization, there are any number of words and phrases for the general belief that nothing happens in the office, no matter how much activity there is. It's like taking Latin when the teacher says that it's "good for you," and someday you will appreciate it. I still don't appreciate it. Few of us mind working toward an objective. None of us like working toward an unclear end or toward an end we know we will never reach.

The phrase that best captures the frustration of being busy accomplishing an unclear goal with little hope of making a contribution is "rotating bald tires." It is a phrase I learned from a group of teamsters in a big trucking company. I've now heard it several times, coined by the lowest level people in an organization I worked with that saw reorganization after reorganization where nothing ever changed. The CEO kept his job, senior execs changed jobs like musical chairs, and there was lots of commotion—but nothing changed.

When bald tires are rotated they end up in different places, but they are the same tires and the vehicle is still dangerous. Nothing has changed. And worse, a lot of work and elbow grease went into rotating them. In an organization, is there anything that conjures up something more futile than the best resources in an organization wasting time? Huge effort is spent every day in making progress in every company, but if nothing changes, no progress is made; it's just like the bald tires. It's even worse if the organization is constrained or people are worried about their jobs. And today, that covers just about every organization. A false sense of activity will keep everyone busy but results will be slim.

Without engaging in buzzword bingo, there is a corollary phrase to "rotating bald tires." It applies when employee teams are helping with a reorganization. That is when I've heard: "we are building our own coffin."

CRITICAL AND CANCEL ARE NOT REDUNDANT

A false sense of activity trickles down from the top and is contagious as it works its way through the system. Others will catch it, and soon the entire staff suffers with this false sense of activity. As in, "I am too busy to even go to the bathroom. I am not sure if my work matters that much but I need to keep up this façade of busyness!"

Imagine this real conversation at home after George puts in a long day at the "mill:"

"Honey, we need to cancel our vacation because I'm worried about my job. They announced another cost-cutting and process-improvement project today that will affect my department. There are consultants all over the place running around like bumper cars. I know they are there to cut jobs."

Spouse: "Oh, George, we were all so looking forward to our vacation. The kids have been packing their little suitcases for weeks. Can't you do anything to fix it?"

George: "No, and what makes it even more infuriating is that even though I know the company is in trouble, I spend most of my day doing bullshit work that I know no one will ever care about or see. I waste my time and I'm worried the most when I know I should be doing more important work. Even the managers are hanging around and spending their time on things that they know won't improve the place. They are just as frustrated as we are. That CEO doesn't know what the hell he is doing."

VACATIONS ARE NOT SINS

Hello? George? Hello? CEO?

I would guess that George is going to lose his job whether he takes his vacation or not, so he may as well take it. Anyone like George who is worried about his job probably should be. Who knows better than George whether or not he is making a contribution? Who knows better than George where he sits politically in the company? And who knows better than George where he sits in the pecking order of who or what will be cut? If you're worried about your job, you probably should be looking for another job. Here's my advice:

- George, take the vacation. Don't disappoint the kids based on something that may or may not happen. In any case, you don't have any control over the outcome, and the chances are very good that the lack of priorities and focus will still be there when you return.

- CEO, you have bigger problems than communications—but start there. Give people time frames for change, if change is happening. There is usually no confusion about what we are changing from, but there is always confusion about what we are changing to. Don't frighten people into canceling vacations due to lack of direction or worry about job security. People remember cancelled vacations forever and will curse you as a sinner forever more.

- George and CEO, remember that those who take vacations are more productive, and more productive people make better organizations.

The Benefits of Taking Vacations

According to a May 21, 2007, *Business Week* article:

"The vanishing vacation has many perils. Refusing to take time off burns people out and wreaks havoc on productivity." The article goes on to quote a study conducted by Families & Work Institute that identifies over-working as one reason employees report more mistakes and behave angrily towards their co-workers.

Former NASA scientists, working on behalf of Air New Zealand and using testing tools that were developed for astronauts, recently found that employees who took vacations experienced an 82 percent increase in their job performances when they returned. Two or three days off unfortunately does not deliver the same stress-reduction benefits as vacations of one and two weeks, other research shows. Experts agree that most of us need a dramatic change of scenery and extensive relaxation to renew our focus and efficacy. We are, in effect, like cell phones. We need to be charged up.

"Making yourself available 24/7 does not create peak performance," says psychiatrist Edward Hallowell, an instructor at Harvard Medical School. "Recreating the boundaries that technology has eroded does."

If you take away nothing more from this book, remember to take vacations that you are due. The issues and opportunities will all still be there when you return. CEOs take vacations. Some take lots of them.

INACTIVITY AND LOOKING FOR THE BIG PICTURE

The excuse for committing the sin of inactivity is often about the lack of any overriding big goal, or big picture within the organization. The absence of the goal leads to a false sense of activity or just plain inactivity.

The "big picture" is one of those phrases that floats from corporate offices to every office and plant. It comes back to roost when someone asks, "What is the big picture? I want to know it so I can make decisions." The big picture should define the company goals and mission. At least, it should answer the question: "On what do we base our decisions around here?" Instead, the "big picture" often is framed by obscurity and is, in fact, one of the hardest things for anyone in a company to actually picture. All that the picture needs to do is help people make decisions and understand to what end they are working.

"People above me keep telling me to think in terms of the big picture and to inspire my group to function the same way. But ask anyone anyplace in the company what that big picture is and no one can tell you," says Willa, who has a title with a lot of words and acronyms in it. Willa takes her work seriously, but she sees the foibles of the 20,000-employee international company that produces business forms.

"I'm always guessing and hoping my instincts are right. Then just when I think I've got it right, that I'm operating in a way that contributes to securing what it is I last heard is our market niche, someone makes a big speech, and it seems like he's saying something completely different from what some other bigwig said in the company newspaper a month or a week ago.

"I see all the slogans on the wall and the Lucite cubes that commemorate some deal, but as they say on The View, 'So what, who cares!'"

Unless you're in the army, you're entitled to a lot more than marching orders. Employees have a right to feel part of something bigger than their day-to-day tasks. The most satisfied groups know that what they do meshes with the overall goals of the company. Leaders need to find one or make it up, or sins result. It can always be changed.

TEMPTATION

The "vision thing" is tricky. Some leaders think it is a waste of time and energy. If there isn't that "thing," no one will care. The temptation is to ignore it.

George H. W. Bush, the first Bush president, never wanted to create or bother with what he called "the vision thing" when he was in office, and he was lambasted for it. But think about the one question that is most often used to evaluate our political leaders. The question that is attributed to the leadership or lack thereof is captured in, "Is the country headed in the right direction?" If the response is not good, leadership is in trouble. A positive response means all is well. The question itself implies that there is a direction, when there is no direction. Watch out on election day because people will remember that sin. George Bush The First was not re-elected.

Great leaders are remembered for their "big picture." Martin Luther King talked literally about his dream, his vision. John Kennedy is always cited for his vision to put a man on the moon. Conversely, look at those who are not seen as great leaders, and almost always there will be a lack of a vision. Big sin.

Lou Gerstner is credited with saving IBM from going out of business in the early 1990s. He claimed he was not interested in the vision thing either. In reality, the first thing he did was create a vision. Instead of breaking the company into "Baby Blues," he kept the company together and focused on IT services, the internet, and reviving the company's culture. He created the vision by what he did and how he made decisions. He didn't have to create wall posters. No sin.

A big reason I always appreciate the big picture is that it creates choices for everyone in the organization. If you don't agree with the big picture, at least you have the choice of leaving or staying.

The Big Picture: Little Sins

- **Whining.** Don't whine about the "lack of a big picture." There are probably clues all around that can help you discover it.

- **Ignoring the Three-Things Rule.** Every employee in every organization in the world wants to know three things: what's my job, how am I doing, and how does my job relate to the big picture? Clarify all three as the leader, or define them yourself if no one is helping you.

- **Seeking Perfection.** Getting to 80 percent right may be as good as it gets. The big picture may not always be clear or constant, but if everyone knows the variables that affect it, people's tolerance for ambiguity will increase. Everyone will appreciate *good enough*.

- **Setting unreal expectations.** Big pictures are rarely as grandiose as we've hoped or imagined. Nor will they answer all our questions about the organizational direction. Get over it.

The Nub of the Sin

The core of the sin of paralysis lies in the personal choices we make every day, often simple ones about setting priorities and goals and strategies for achieving them. To not make those choices, however small they may seem, means we choose inaction. Even when there is a lack of clarity about priorities, we can make educated guesses. The core of this sin is waiting for definition rather than taking the hints and acting upon them.

The CEO Banker: A Trick Question?

During a new business proposal at a major bank I watched the CEO fiddling with his pencil and gazing into the distance. His thoughts were elsewhere, and I was wondering why we were all wasting our time if he had no interest in the proposal. Everyone could sense the lack of interest so it was a gloomy hour. As we were wrapping up the presentation and shaking hands to say good-bye, he stopped and said, "Hold on, I have a question for you that could turn into an assignment." Hope sprang eternal. "My question is, Why don't poor people have bank accounts?" There was silence in the room as we all wondered if it was a trick question.

It was not a trick question. Turns out poor people don't like to go into banks. But they will happily open an account in the lobby of a grocery store or in other easy places. The bank changed direction on a dime to open tiny branches everywhere, and the growth strategy for the bank became very clear.

Many jobs nowadays are designed so they are never done, never complete. They are more of a continuum of activities where there may never be a concrete result. Draining e-mail and voicemail all day is almost always a set of defensive tasks to keep you out of trouble and keep you from knowing where you're supposed to go. Yet, all of these activities represent choices.

Choosing a box of laundry detergent means picking among boxes labeled jumbo, family size, extra large, or giant. When ordering a simple cardboard cup of coffee, we can choose a large, grande, or el supremo. These days it seems our lives in the workplace are full of similar choices that range from "This is critical to the project, and jobs are at stake" to "This is urgent and must be completed by end of week." to "Do this ASAP."

Finishing the ASAPs usually only gets you to the place where the real work is waiting. Lots of times, that's the work that never gets done. That gnawing feeling you get when you leave at the end of the day is from all that work that you didn't even get to see. It's a world of nebulous defeats.

Many of the successful people I know are adept at converting those nebulous defeats into ambiguous victories. Some are able to turn those defeats into clear victories. The secret is not denial and quiet suffering. The secret is perspective and an absolute focus on setting priorities.

AMBIGUOUS VICTORIES

A CEO of a major telecommunications company was faced with a workforce about to go on strike, a backlog of installations, a reorganization that was going over like a joke told in poor taste, and dissatisfied customers everywhere he looked. When faced with this reality he said with a big sigh, "It's only dial tone." He knew that with a good dose of perspective and some creative solutions, he would extricate himself from the malaise of an organization mired in nebulous defeats. He did.

Maybe he asked himself, "What's the worst that can happen to me?" And his answer of "probably not that much" gave him confidence to keep at it and prevail. Maybe he recognized that "dial tone" is not on a par with a cure for world hunger, and that he could make things work if he stayed with it. Maybe he went into his figurative "cave" and came out with a big solution and the tactics to back it up. In any case, he chose to make things better. He set very clear objectives and did not waiver from them. His mantra was, "We may not be right, but we're not confused." What seemed like nebulous defeats on that one bad day became ambiguous victories in a short time.

CREATING VICTORIES: THE CEO IN THE PARKING LOT

Paul is a CEO of a major manufacturing company who is trying to make big changes. "By the time I became the CEO of such a big company, I didn't think that I would have to worry about these kinds of issues," he told me. He was the number-one guy at a company with 90,000 people—large, by any measure. He was making changes as to how the company was organized, how it treated its customers, how it would develop products, and how many people it would employ. The people in the company had heard about imminent changes forever but nothing had really ever changed. It was starting to look like this time could be different—change really would happen—and everyone could tell. Paul was starting to feel some personal pressure—not about the changes, but about how he was viewed. The "issues" he was dealing with were about him:

"We had our consultants help determine what changes we should make and assess how the employees were reacting to the changes. When the consultants presented their results, the only thing I heard was that the people who work here hate me," he reported. "They believe it is their God-given right to work here and that I was changing that right. The consultants told me that it was so bad that if the employees saw me in the parking lot they would speed up to hit me. With 90,000 people and a lot of parking lots that really got my attention.

"It's important for me to be liked, but it's more important for me to make what I think are the right moves for us. Even though they say they don't like me they also say they don't know me. I'm not sure what they want to know about me because it's not all that interesting. I am not a rock star, but somehow they have it in their minds that I need to be like Jack Welch or Bill Gates or Mick Jagger.

"The satellite down-linked telecasts weren't enough. The phone-mail messages to all employees weren't enough. Communications was always the first problem that showed up on all of our employee surveys. Everyone told me I had to go out—so out I went and held a bunch of meetings with employees all over the country. It was painful. In every single presentation there was a self-appointed spokesperson who would ask a question about layoffs. It usually went something like this: 'I've only been here for twenty years but there are a lot of people in this room who have been here for up to thirty-five years. Are you telling me that we all might show up one day and that could be our last?' There is no way to answer that question. They may as well ask me when I stopped beating my wife.

"It was important that I tell them the financial picture of the company and why specific changes were necessary. I felt a little like a teacher or salesman with pie charts and graphs, but it is the only way I know how to talk to groups. Although each meeting was a little bit different, I thought that I had met the need that they needed to know me. Even though I thought the meetings were successful, I always ran through the parking lots. Never can tell who has a car idling out there to hit me.

"Now I hear that maybe the meetings weren't so successful. They thought that my charts with the numbers were too complicated and went over their heads. Even though I was talking about the financial performance of the company, something they should all care about, they thought I was only explaining my stock options. Another criticism was that I came out there with expensive $500 suits and a limo driver. They should know how much my suits really cost, and that I have a driver not as a luxury but so that I can talk on the phone and look at numbers at the same time. Now I hear they want me to 'shoot' my driver. I guess if I drove up in a Ford Pinto they would criticize me for not acting like a CEO. And if I fired the driver they would really go crazy for the way I treat people.

"So let me get this straight. I'm an asshole if I don't go out and talk to employees because they believe I don't care. But if I do go out and talk to people all they focus on are my suits and my limo driver.

"What I am going to do is ignore all this noise. I know what I have to do and I am going to do it. My mother told me that every day is a gift, and I am going to treat every day here that way. We are going to change and I am going to lead it."

This CEO was right and is still a successful executive. He knew the workforce would be won over and would create a successful company. In the meantime, he was going to convert the losses into victories. He did.

I shared his thought about every day being a gift, but at the same time, worried about those 90,000 people with cars. As uncomfortable as it was at first, especially in parking lots, he chose not to be defeated by something as fickle as morale. He worked the morale issue by "getting out there with the people" and eventually created a victory. His attention to creating goals and sticking with them allowed for the ambiguous victories. He did this by setting up a series of creative algorithms.

Algorithms are a basic tenet of math, and this CEO created a constant set of algorithms that made sense. The algorithms were a simple and never ending set of IF/THEN equations. As in, "IF we improve margins, THEN there will be no layoffs. IF we introduce the new product before year-end, THEN there will be bonuses." People believed him and there was a happy ending all around.

Choosing to make things different is what separates that nebulous defeat from the ambiguous victory and inhibits paralysis. That choice is yours.

I have seen in leaders that the commitment to constantly choose is as liberating as the choices. Making the commitment to choose all the time is the surrogate for closure that we long for.

ACTION VS. INACTION: WHAT IS REAL WORK?

In these uncertain times everyday events can easily be interpreted as nebulous defeats. The uncertainty is about much more than the economic future or the latest news on the war against terrorism. The uncertainty seems to rotate around every decision we make, every day, because there are so many of them. It can be paralyzing. As the number of choices increases, so does the potential for nebulous defeats. The volume and types of decisions that must be made make these uncertain times. Ambiguity can lead to the inactivity sin, so let's try to adjust the ambiguity by answering some questions I have heard of late about inaction.

Am I doing my real work? (I wasn't hired to do this.) If you never get to your "real work," maybe what you are doing *is* your real work, and there is no reason to despair over what is or isn't getting done. Feel good about what does get done and how it contributes to some goal, although it may not have been yours.

Should I suffer with an old computer (cell phone, car, golf clubs, gizmos) or get a new one? Suffering can lead to inactivity. Don't be a sinner.

Should I work from home so I can be near my kids or go to an office? Kids mean having a crazy calendar and being very active but not sure being around them helps finish projects. If you can be productive from home—between dropping off kids, dogs barking, UPS deliveries, leaf blowers, and other distractions—go for it.

Should I take call-waiting while I'm on the phone with my boss? No. Bosses have very keen antennae when it comes to inactivity. There are more important calls than your boss but not that many. Also, don't paste or tweet your location for your boss to see.

Should I travel to the meeting or try to participate remotely? Tricky question. To put it another way I've heard, "Should I fly for six hours and be mostly inactive for a one-hour meeting?" Depending on what is at stake, the answer is often yes.

Should I miss the meeting and go to the soccer game? Learn how to use the mute button well and call in.

Should I do ten things at once and move them all forward a little bit or pick one and finish it? Better to finish a big thing. While choosing to not be inactive, do the little things.

Should I eat that Krispy Kreme donut? Since it's free, will it be less fattening? Nothing makes you more inactive than Krispy Kremes.

Every day, all day, each of us is faced with decisions, large and small. Making effective choices that create closure inherently prevents paralysis.

~~~~~~

Paralysis Indicators

- False sense of activity: Always busy, but nothing ever seems to get done.

- Strategic Plan is 300 pages long: Some leaders can put the plan for the organization on a cocktail napkin.

- All-nighters all the time: Like juggling chainsaws, there is always a crisis a flip away if it isn't done tonight.

- Organization chart mania: More attention paid to the org chart than to getting things done.

- Toxic workplace: Pressured environment with lots of yelling. If everyone is playing a guessing game about what is important, people will be wrong a lot, which means an unhappy world of cubicles.

- Complicated diagrams full of arrows and dotted lines that illustrate the business model, but still no one understands what it is.

 REDEMPTION

Redemption of paralysis occurs when something—sometimes anything—moves forward.

Move Something Forward

Take action. Inertia is a powerful drug. It is both addictive and contagious to those around you. Combat it, even if the action you take feels unnecessary or contrived. It's a sign of life in a dead zone. A paralyzed CEO will preside over a paralyzed organization.

Know Thyself and plan accordingly

A little self-awareness can prevent paralysis. Some leaders and managers thrive when they move a thousand things an inch forward over the course of a month. Others want to move two things a mile over the course of a month. Knowing which type you are will help you set plans and create closure.

Takeaways

At first glance, paralysis is a sin that doesn't seem to apply today. How can we be paralysed when we enjoy such advanced technology and productivity tools—and when we obsess about keeping our jobs in hard times? Paralysis seems counterintuitive. Nonetheless, the sin of paralysis and its resulting inactivity persist in our high-tech times, hurting individual careers and organization performance.

Here are some ways to stay clear of it:

- **Avoid the victim syndrome.** Those who feel paralyzed often feel like the victim of the actions, or lack thereof, of those around them. Yet, as Christopher Reeve said, "Paralysis is an individual choice."

- **Take small steps.** No one sits down and writes a novel. Even great authors sit down and write a word, a sentence, a paragraph, and a chapter that will eventually become parts of that novel. Make a small movement out of paralysis by doing something as simple as checking off a few things on the To Do list.

- **Take a risk.** Sometimes the first step out of paralysis is taking the risk of actually doing what you thought you were not able to do.

- **Motivate yourself.** Think of anything that will break the inertia and act as an incentive. A raise? Promotion? Pride? The list of possibilities is endless.

- **Set priorities.** Set your own priorities, then assess how they'll serve you and the organization.

And remember, always …
When everything is critical, nothing is important.

5

THE SIN: CLUELESSNESS

"That Can't Be Me!"

At a trade show I attended not long ago, I saw Joe, a CEO I really respected, smoking pot with a customer in a hotel hallway. Employees from Joe's company were all around watching him. He didn't last on his job much longer after that.

Another chief executive of a large telecommunications company, Pete, was checking out the latest in pornography on the web using his company-issued computer connected to the company server. Not bad enough, he decided to send some of the same juicy material to some of his friends, still using that company hardware. When the board lowered the boom on him, Pete was surprised and wasn't sure what he had done wrong. No one bothered to explain it to him later. The attitude was, he should have known.

I wonder, is it me or are these guys clueless about how their actions reflect on them and their organization? Will they ever see the errors of their ways? How close are you to committing some of the crimes of just plain being oblivious? But wait, it gets better!

A young analyst was casually working with me in my office on a budget planning project. It is a task that never ends, and the words budget and planning next to each other are often an oxymoron.

Neither of us ever approached the project with relish so any distraction was welcome, including just watching the comings and goings of the people as they drove up to the building complex. The office building where we were sitting, trying to avoid the project, is typical of Silicon Valley and so many suburban settings—a series of low-slung building connected by parking lots. The young analyst was looking out the window of our building into the parking lot and blinked a few times before she half wondered, half asked, "Are those guys out there smoking dope?" Now she had my attention, and she was more alert than she had been all morning.

It was 11:00 am and I followed her gaze. "Looks like it," I said as they passed around a joint and yukked it up.

"I didn't know anyone did that anymore at this time of day," she said with some casual allusion to college that made me wonder.

CEOs: Dazed and Confused

Sure enough, there were three guys out there in the bright morning sun, each about thirty years old, all wearing black suits with no ties, standing around a car and enjoying the moment. Our low-slung building had black glass so we could see out but no one could see in, so we watched and made up stories about them.

Maybe one was smoking for medicinal purposes and the others were joining in as a show of support. Ha Ha. Maybe they were part of a Mexican drug cartel and the venture capital firm next door was their main channel of distribution. LOL. Maybe they were the custodians in the buildings and had been stealing office supplies for years to support their habit. Now they were showing us their new suits. Ha Ha Ha.

"I would guess they must be really nervous about something. Wish them luck," my friendly analyst finally said, and we went back to the dreaded spreadsheets at hand. We both chuckled and thought little more about it. Shortly, we adjourned, I went back to draining email, and my trusty analyst went back to all the things analysts do every day in a sea of cubes.

Ten minutes later, the receptionist buzzed me for my next appointment. As I walked into the conference room, sure enough, there were the same three guys from the parking lot. The three were the CEO, the chief marketing guy, and the chief technology guy. I made no indication at all that I had seen them in the parking lot. What would I have said? Since they were making a pitch for a big money investment, maybe they really were trying to calm their nerves. They were looking for eight million dollars to build out their video game company that had some success already with thirty employees. Now everyone in the office knew what had happened in the parking lot. The power of the informal network is strong. It was an immediate joke in the office, and the executive assistants were coming in and out offering the guests candy bars and munchies. One EA brought in tissues and Visine in case they had eyestrain. It was hard to sit through the meeting and not ask about judgment and habits, or say, "Did it ever occur to you that people might be watching you through a window as you were getting stoned?"

The question in my mind as I sat there was not even about the pot. It was not a moral or legal dilemma. The question was about the judgment of people who would stand out in the parking lot in plain sight smoking dope right before what might be the most important meeting in the life of the company. Did they think no one would notice? Did they think it was OK? Did they think it would help their performance? The guys left, did not get their eight million dollars, and probably never knew why. At least they probably got to laugh about the meeting afterwards.

MIND-ALTERING SUBSTANCES NOT REQUIRED

Many leaders don't need mind-altering substances to commit the sin of being clueless. The video game leaders would have been oblivious somewhere else, if not in the parking lot. Maybe some leaders are missing a gene that makes them know what is going on around them. Maybe if they opened their eyes, looked around, and recognized the situation surrounding them, they would not demonstrate the sin of being oblivious so readily. It happens every day in big and small ways.

I have heard CEOs give major speeches with some annoying and distracting audio problem that persists through the entire talk. Rather than stop and ask, "What the hell is that noise?" they drone on while no one in the audience pays any attention. The CEO's message is lost, other than the audience believing the speaker is oblivious to his surroundings.

I have seen PowerPoint presentations with lots of slides where the leader/presenter introduces each slide with the disclaimer, "I know you can't read this, but …" and then drones on while no one pays attention to something that they cannot see. I have seen a CEO who makes millions of dollars give a presentation to a crowd of hip media types while he was wearing shabby clothes that did not fit. His hairy belly could be seen between the buttons of a bulging dress shirt. Everyone noticed his belly and his lack of understanding of what was going on around him and wondered what he was doing with his money. Like the guys smoking pot, these CEOs were oblivious as well. And the question of their judgment enters here too. Did they think people wouldn't notice?

Mr. Hipster

"There was a band in the '60s named the Rolling Stones. Anyone ever hear of them?" So asked a CEO at a marketing meeting as he announced a new theme song. The audience all rolled their eyes and assumed he'd just heard of the Rolling Stones himself.

SOCIAL NETWORKS AND CEO SINS

Leaders are never off duty. None of us are ever off duty today. As one leader put it, "What used to be ways to capture memories are now ways to capture evidence." Drunken weekend forays that show up on YouTube count, and go on the permanent record. Given the nature of social networks and the pervasiveness of videos, we are all on duty all the time, no matter what our role or company level. The sin of being oblivious is not reserved for leaders.

CEOs: VIDEO ON DEMAND

A reporter for the *Wall Street Journal* called me about a situation involving video. There was an event at a big company, and the reporter was asking what the CEO should do. The situation was this: A vice president of sales was conducting his weekly meeting with the sales staff. It was routine, like the thousands of Monday staff meetings held throughout the world each week. There were at least 100 sales people in the room, including some recent college graduates.

The VP ranted about sales quotas with phrases like, "Anyone who doesn't exceed goals this week—I'll fire their ass!" and "I am goddamn tired of having to go to the CEO and make excuses. I am tired of this shit and I will dog all of you until you make me look good!" The room was silent and very uncomfortable to say the least.

We have all been to that meeting. What the ranting lunatic didn't know was that a technically astute sales rep in the crowd was recording the diatribe on a cell phone. Later that day, with the company logo prominently featured, the video showed up on YouTube for the world to see the sales VP in all his glory. The question from the reporter was, "What should the CEO do?"

If a mirror were held up to the oblivious sales guy, and maybe to a similarly oblivious CEO in the same organization, their response would be, "that can't be me." It is. And, the mirror doesn't have to be held up; the YouTube video is there as the mirror.

When any CEO or any manager is oblivious, everyone knows. Obliviousness is worse when the CEO believes he is on top of things and not oblivious. Think Michael Scott on *The Office*. Even when situations are brought to the CEO's attention, obliviousness may continue. It's like the sin of being oblivious squared.

Oblivion is Not Bliss

Consultants are often messengers to leaders. The thinking is we will still have a job tomorrow, regardless of the message we deliver. People inside organizations don't have that freedom. So a software developer at a telecommunications company handed me a message and asked me to deliver it to the CEO. He knew I had access and asked me not to reveal the source.

The developer fits the profile for what many consider to be typical for that job: never wears a tie; works irregular hours often long in the night; has a cluttered cube that includes his bike and trendy doodads. Developers are known to speak irreverently of corporate policies and traditions. This guy loves the technology that he works on, and he cares for the company a great deal although he may not be demonstrative in that regard. The thought of changing companies is disturbing because he is in the middle of a project that he believes is important. He likes his work. And, he would have to move his stuff. He would tell you that money isn't important to him since he is an "artist." If it was, he would be working for a start-up with the possibility of stock options even though those aren't worth what they used to be.

"I can't connect the dots here," is his usual refrain.

He is struggling to make logical connections between the company's performance and the actions the CEO is taking and the messages he is delivering. What he keeps asking himself is:

"If we're doing so well under trying conditions—or as the CEO says, 'We are on track and meeting our adjusted plan'—why do I feel like we are losing ground? Since we're working so hard on what we are told is an important project, why is my department always chosen for cuts? Why can't I influence someone who looks at the numbers and makes decisions? What I see around me just doesn't make any sense. Leadership always says they want open communications and want to hear from us, and I don't trust that I won't be tracked down if I send it in email, so I am stuck with this anonymous printed note to Bob, the CEO."

So I delivered the note.

Yo, Bob, pay attention please:

I hope that you are reading and truly listening to what I'm saying in this note, for it accurately describes the feelings that many of us "down here" have. To be blunt, we just don't believe anything that management is telling us these days. We can read for ourselves the newsletters and the letters from you in the quarterly and annual reports, and we hear the official party line, but we know it just ain't so.

One in three people in my department was laid off last week but all the work is still here. Come down and see it sometime. When I look at the grossly high (relative to other companies like us) executive salaries/bonuses/stocks/loans, the profitable last Quarter, million dollar executive severance packages, and billions in the bank, I find if difficult to accept the notion that we are in serious financial trouble. If we are, how can we pay big hiring bonuses and some of our executives over two million a year? If we are in financial trouble, other than the profits, tell me again whose mistake it was? Hmmmm? Was it the employees who were laid off? Or was it, just possibly, the executives and high level managers of this company? Not including you, of course. Tell me again, who it is that is paying for all the mistakes with the job losses and work getting piled on?

Sorry Bob, whenever I try to swallow the party line on this one, I just keep gagging. Please don't be clueless.

Signed,

A loyal employee down here

Who is not in favor of the new slogan: The Future Is Here!

Now what?

This leader has a choice: tune in or check out; assume responsibility or assume the charge of being clueless.

TEMPTATION

The CEO can be tempted into oblivion. We are all tempted by the "How was I supposed to know?" rule. Here's a Symptoms' Checklist for the rationales of cluelessness:

> —Maybe if no one tells me about it, I won't know about it and won't have to deal with it.
> —Maybe if I am oblivious to it, I won't have to deal with it.
> —Maybe if I don't pay attention to it, it will go away.
> —Maybe the people are oblivious about how hard this job is.
> —Maybe no one will know where I am and what I am doing.

Succumbing to the sin only leads to trouble.

The former CEO of BP, Tony Hayward, may become the poster child for the sin of being oblivious. His comment, "I want my life back," put him in the crosshairs of all the suffering Gulf Coast residents. Regardless of his actions up to that time, he was oblivious to the sting of that remark and its repercussions. When he later showed up on the yacht club circuit, the sin was only compounded. The sin of being oblivious cost him his job.

When the Governor of South Carolina, Mark Sanford, disappeared for a few days to meet a woman in South America, he seemed oblivious to his actions and the consequences in so many ways. Anyone who disappears from any job at any level with no explanation for a few days is in trouble. You will either be fired or have the police looking for you. A high school student with a part-time minimum wage job at a fast food chain knows this. A high-ranking public official? It's an entirely different league of committing the sin of being oblivious. There is no license to be oblivious no matter the rank.

How'm I Doing?

When it comes to their own performance, CEOs can be the most oblivious:

The board of directors at a midsized tech company had been frustrated with the performance of the company for some time. Inherent in the performance of the company was the performance of the CEO. His presentations full of numbers in parentheses and red ink were a surefire way to attract attention. Comments like, "You have to fix this next quarter," or "The competition is not hurting like this … what is happening here?" were common at board meetings. But nothing ever happened. The board finally pulled the trigger to fire the CEO. When confronted with his imminent unemployment, the CEO was shocked and started yelling at the chairperson and threatening lawsuits. No wonder he was being fired we all thought—How could he be so oblivious?

Being oblivious to one's own performance is a particularly curious sin because common sense dictates that, in general, people can accurately assess their own performance. The key phrase here is "in general." While I watching a youth soccer game recently, a boy who was maybe five years old ran out of the game declaring, "I sucked!" Immediately, a group of adults coddled him and said, "No, you were great, Johnnie." But I had been watching other players beat Johnnie to the ball and score around him. The other kids were laughing at him. Johnnie was right—he had sucked, and he had accurately assessed his performance. When I give a speech, I feel a sense of how I performed. When I handle a situation, I have some sense of the efficacy of my approach. Of course, what I tell my boss or my wife about it may be different, but in my heart of hearts, I think I know. The sports metaphors for this hypothesis are legion.

CEOs know how they are performing. The belief that we are pretty good at knowing our own and others' performances fueled the outrage over the bonuses paid out during the latest financial meltdown. If everyone knows the performances of the execs at AIG sucked, *they* must know too, so how can they accept those big bonuses in good conscience? A surefire path to the kingdom of sins.

It's All Good

When a CEO asks for feedback about his performance, he may really be looking for affirmation, not criticism. The common problem is affirmation is exactly what he gets. When your spouse comes out of the bathroom and asks, "How do I look?" be careful before you say anything other than "terrific!" After a speech, when your boss asks you, "How did I do?" only say it was a bomb if you have another job lined up. Don't believe me; try giving negative feedback in either situation.

Of course there are exceptions to the rule. There are those people who honestly want feedback, but those are often the people who want to move their performance from a level 8 to a level 10. Then there are those who know how poorly they performed but may want to be told they performed really well anyway.

The reality could be poor financial results, tainted products, or employees that don't care about results. In short, the future of the organization will disintegrate based on a CEO who chooses to be, or who just is, oblivious.

Too Much Time at the Desk

At an executive staff meeting I listened as a brand new CEO described events in his office over the weekend. "Since I spend so much time in my office, away from my wife, we have a tradition. When I assume a new role we come into the office over the weekend and have sex on my desk. That way she is always here with me. It was great." The staff looked at him in disbelief before they stared at the desk. No one said a word, but they wondered how clueless he was about how often anyone wanted to sit across the desk from him.

Think You're Clueless?—Ask people

Like the holiday party, employee surveys are an annual event in some organizations. Any leader who wants to know how they are perceived is sure to be interested in the employee survey. The surveys are loathed by some and enjoyed by others (usually those who vilify management), but surveys always receive a lot of attention. In every survey ever conducted at any organization a key deficiency that always requires improvement is "communications"—as in, "Communications around here sucks." "Communications" is often a code word for confusion, for an atmosphere in which no one can separate the critical from the important.

I helped administer the first employee survey at Apple Computer. It was where I first heard the phrase "false sense of activity," which expressed the biggest frustration there at the time. I have since learned that this particular sin pervades high-tech companies. When everyone is so, so busy, a simple decision that might take five minutes is delayed because the decision maker is too busy. Everything is ASAP or critical, and yet nothing gets done. The line between committing the sin of waffling or the sin of being oblivious is thin.

Sometimes being oblivious leads to waffling and vice versa.

Even at innovative and focused companies like Apple, the survey is one of the best ways for leaders to understand what is going on. The survey can potentially cure oblivion by shedding light on problems and perceptions of the corporate culture. But surveys are useless unless their findings are integrated into policy. And they're special, not designed to be completed every day.

IS BEING CLUELESS DANGEROUS?

Recent brain research suggests that parts of the teenage brain are underdeveloped. The research specifically finds that the part used for judgment and awareness is the same size as that of a small rodent. Having dealt with four teenage children, I think that might be an optimistic estimate. Regarding some CEOs, the research might point to parallels between typical teenager and CEO behavior. Or as a customer service rep claimed in describing the company's CEO, "How can he be that oblivious and still be alive after all these years?" Like teenagers, CEOs can believe that rules are for others and do their damnedest to test boundaries. And, like teenagers, some leaders take risks without understanding the consequences and are clueless as to the repercussions of foolish actions.

Also like teenagers, CEOs often cannot help being clueless, but they can be trained to take crucial facts into account. There are just a few simple credos to follow:

1. **Always let someone know where you are. And be there.**

2. **Never assume you have permission because you explained what you are going to do.** Caveat for both groups: Acting in a good way without permission can still be the way to go.

3. **Be home when you say you will be home.**

4. **Know that there are some rules that are absolutely non-negotiable.** For the teenager it could be "Give me the keys." For the leader the rule might be, "Never, ever, do anything that you wouldn't want on the front page of the *Wall Street Journal*."

5. If you're in deep trouble, don't negotiate. It will only get worse. Don't be oblivious to the consequence of the action.

The temptation for the CEO is to believe that being oblivious lets him off the responsibility hook. Ignorance for a CEO is not bliss, it is a sin, and cluelessness is even worse.

 TEMPTATION

In Defense of the Clueless

Here is why oblivion may be so ubiquitous in senior management, and for CEOs in particular:

- There is not always a logical explanation between what we see and what the organization must do. Ask anyone who has to deal with airline schedules. Being stranded in Dallas because of a snow storm in Detroit it may stretch your logic. The same is true when the leader has to make a decision in marketing based on lack of performance in engineering. The CEO has to make those counterintuitive connections.

- Companies sometimes do have to cut costs even when things seem to be going well. It may seem crazy, because it kills morale and loyalty, but it may prevent further cuts later. Then again, it may not.

- There is no relationship between executive pay and other events in the company. Look at executive pay levels the same way you look at baseball player salaries, or it will make you crazy.

~~~~~~

Only 2 Percent Oblivious

It was an extravaganza for the big apparel company, an all-hands meeting in the lobby of the corporate headquarters. There were spotlights and loud music blaring as everyone walked into the auditorium. The people liked these meetings because food and wine were served and everyone got to see and mingle with professional models as they sashayed around in the full regalia of next season's offerings. There were models and a runway and a new apparel line that was about to be launched. It was corporate rock and roll. Shortly after the supermodels finished the strut, the CEO stood up and said he was looking for a good next year, not great. And, because of that, most people would receive a less than 2 percent raise next year. After all the models and the music and the product pronouncements, everyone left the meeting muttering about the 2 percent.

~~~~~~

CLUELESS BELOW THE WAIST?

There is a connection between cluelessness and sex, and the stories of the link between the two are endless and relate to almost every other sin. Leaders are always on stage. Being "on" all the time is just a part of the price one pays for the perks of leadership. To think otherwise is to be clueless. So any indiscretion or boorish behavior is sure to be observed and sure to lead to problems. The question to always ask is, "How will this look to the outside world?" Those who work around a CEO are rarely clueless if something is going on.

The sex connection is only one of many ways where behaviors reflect on the leader, and leaders cannot be clueless as to what that means. The CEO who treats receptionists or parking attendants like dirt will be seen as a jerk. The one who takes private jets while others fly coach will be seen as extravagant. The one who is not in his office much will be regarded as absent and hence, clueless.

Cluelessness is a trait in a leader that sticks. Dan Quayle is an example. Former Vice President Quayle is probably smart and aware but through a series of gaffes (like spell potato?) and actions, he was labeled clueless and never recovered.

Clueless Indicators

- **Feedback.** Always asking for feedback from those who will say only good things. The term for such adoring fans is "sycophants." A more truthful feedback provider is usually a spouse or kids.

- **Snickering.** When the leader walks into the conference room and gentle giggling ensues, everyone knows something that he should know too.

- **Awkward situations.** Think dunk tank. The leader who puts himself in a position that will allow others to see him as clueless *is* clueless.

 REDEMPTION

"Get a clue!" might be the most appropriate way to steer clear of this sin.

Getting that clue might be as simple as truly opening our eyes and ears, walking halls, showing up, reading reports, paying attention in meetings, and being on "red alert" when it comes to sexual behavior and rumor.

Seeing and hearing what's going on around the organization shouldn't be so hard. If you can't do that, listen to surveys conducted by truthful consultants. They will tell you how clueless you might be. The simple act of treating everyone in the organization with care and respect can cure the sin of cluelessness. The "little people" can make life miserable, or make a difference.

CEOs are supposed to be self-aware, and the most successful ones that I've known have a keen understanding of their role and impact. The good ones are not clueless.

Takeaways

- "Clueless" is never a compliment. Think Homer Simpson. Think Michael Scott on *The Office*. Anyone labeled "clueless" will find it difficult to throw off the moniker, whether it's accurate or not. Think Dan Quayle.

- Never act like the protagonist in the Hans Christian Andersen tale of *The Emperor's New Clothes*. Being the organizational emperor might seem like a safe place for the CEO, but not for long. Eventually someone will say he has no clothes. No one ever said it was an easy job so why not take advantage of the role? Be the emperor with the clothes!

- As in high school, simply do the required homework.

- Data can help cure cluelessness. If there is a lot of judgment involved in determining the truth, explaining the data behind the judgment can keep everyone out of the cluelessness closet.

- Listen to the right people and build their trust. Key contacts can reveal what's happening under the radar and make suggestions before the fires need to be extinguished.

Part Two

AGGRESSIVE SINNERS

(Sins of Commission)

6

THE SIN: FIBBING

A Few Small Repairs Is All We Need

One of the "rise and fall" stories of all time in business is the story of Atari. Once upon a time, Atari was one of Silicon Valley's original successes. The growth of the company was astronomical and unheard of at the time—1981. I was there, for the rise and the fall. Atari was the first Google, Facebook, or eBay, and there were lessons galore to be learned. There were lessons about leadership and planning and controls, to name a few. But the big lesson to be learned was about avoiding the truth.

I stopped telling Atari stories because no one believed them. But here's one that still resonates.

It was at an off-site planning meeting, what else? The CEO was holding court and the top people in the company were all there. A Stanford business school professor was the guest speaker and he said, "Atari will be like the hula hoop. It will be astronomical in its success for a short time, and then it will crash."

There was a stunned silence in the room before someone asked, "What about all those billions of people in China? Don't they need Donkey Kong or Asteroids?" In a minute, everyone piled on with stories of starving peasants in Guatemala and how they were waiting for Ms. Pacman.

It was hard for me to imagine those starving peasants lining up with their quarters to play Centipede, but for the moment my colleagues at Atari had the benefit of the doubt. Driving home that night I was talking to myself about the professor's prediction. Yes, we were sending packages via overnight delivery to the guy in the next cube. Yes, there were no financial controls. Yes, there was an executive dining room with a fancy French chef. Yes, there were a lot of people who had no idea what they were supposed to do when they showed up in the morning. Hey! Maybe the guy was right.

The next day, when the same group reassembled, we were asked about our thoughts again, and once more the discussion, led by the CEO, was about the infinite demand for video games. Who was going to argue with him? So nothing much changed, we kept listening to the CEO's pitch, even though the evidence was to the contrary, and we did become a hula hoop company.

At one time, Atari was the fastest growing company in the world, but one day shortly after that pronouncement about hula hoops by the Stanford professor, the company fired over ten thousand workers, led by the same CEO. He had known the truth and not taken it into account—a major sin. His inability to be honest about the marketplace caused the demise of the company—just as Apple Computer was starting up.

Later, I came to find out that everyone knew the professor was correct at the end of the first day. As we individually drove home that night, we were all muttering to ourselves, "That guy is right. Is anyone going to do anything about it?" We ignored our own thoughts and on that fateful second day, when we could have made course corrections, no one said anything. Just as the CEO had fibbed, we failed to tell the truth to each other and fibbed to ourselves: Maybe we were wrong, we thought. Maybe the company would make it. We avoided the truth. We had collectively and individually committed the sin of fudging. If we learned from it, maybe we could change the way truth would be presented at organizations where we'd work in the future.

TEMPTATION

Big time lies and fraud do take place in organizations. Way too many of them. The sins of Enron, Bernie Madoff, Adelphia, and so many others have been well documented in the courts and in books. You would think the fact that all of these culprits were caught and are paying for their sins would be enough to curtail sinning.

But the lessons are still not getting through. It is easy to see how those sins hurt the employees, shareholders, retirees, communities, and so many others even remotely connected to the companies. Still, there is another sin, maybe less mortal, that does not involve fraud, lying, cheating, and violation of fiduciary responsibility. The sin of denial often leads to the fib, the little white lie, that creates false hope and misdirection in an organization.

What happened in the Atari story was not illegal, but over time the denial and the fibs, as well as other crimes of mismanagement, led to the demise of the company. We all commit the sins of fibbing and avoidance in large and small ways and we all pay for it. Avoidance is often easier than the truth in the short term, but it will kill the organization in the long run.

But It Seemed Like a Good Idea at the Time

As good citizens, the big law firm office had sponsored "Take Your Daughter to Work Day" for years. When it shifted to "Take Your Child to Work Day," the firm stuck with it. The managing partner (the CEO) thought it was good for morale and for the community. His children were too old to be involved, but every year everyone dutifully brought their children in to the office. What the CEO didn't know was that everyone hated the day. The kids didn't want to come because they were with a bunch of other weird kids they didn't know. The lawyers didn't want to bring their kids because they had work to do; they could be annoyed by the kids at home if need be. Most of all, the support staff hated the day because they ended up being babysitters to the brats. After the kids were finished scribbling on the white boards, riding up and down in the elevator while annoying the guards, and getting sick on hot chocolate out of a package, all they wanted to do was play video games, which they could have done at home. Finally, after years of enduring the annual day of torture, someone finally stopped fibbing about how everyone felt about it. The CEO took the occasion to cancel it forevermore.

MINOR SINS ADD UP

Think you never commit the sin of avoidance? Think you never fib or fudge? Think about these questions.

- Is your work-related desktop window open and being ignored while you are secretly bidding on eBay or checking out Facebook? Are you texting your friends while participating in an "important" webinar?

- Do you show up at project planning meetings knowing that someone is not pulling their weight, but you never say anything?

- Do you hate your job but avoid looking for another one because you are "only" twenty years away from retirement?

- Do you avoid asking *really* hard questions like, "Is my job about to be eliminated?"

- Do you avoid doing any real work all day?

- Do you avoid doing any work after 5 PM or on weekends knowing that it will hurt you later? The 9-to-5 day died long ago.

- Do you avoid dealing with the poor performer in the hopes he will find a new job?

- Do you avoid looking at the framed mission statement on the wall because you know it is a lie?

Major Sins Are Killers—Missions Matter

Did you ever wonder if people who work at Phillip Morris smoke cigarettes? If people who work at Nike love to run? Does everyone who works at Electronic Art (EA) love video games? I suspect the answer to all three questions is that people do like to feel connected to the purpose of the organization. So people who think that tobacco is the killer of civilization are the least successful at Phillip Morris; at Nike, those who believe running will kill you don't get promoted; and at EA those who are in the most trouble believe video games are polluting the minds of the youth of the world.

Why an organization exists and what it does are two things that cannot be denied. Yet they are, everyday. At the heart of all organizations lurks a purpose. Sometimes it is difficult to tease out, but it's there. That core needs to be aligned, however tangentially, to something that you can believe in. Something that from time to time makes your heart go pitter-patter. If there is a connection, hallelujah; if not, you are avoiding the truth and committing the sin of denial. "Just a job" can lead to just a small sin.

The Performance Review and Avoidance

The performance review is the Petri dish of lies in all organizations. The review can be the breeding ground of sin. Yes, the review can be an effective tool that helps employees understand how their performance can improve and how their contributions matter. But more often than not, they are like an annual checkup at the dentist—something to be dreaded.

Reviews can be a way of avoiding decisions about who performs well and who "needs improvement." As in, let's just give everyone a "meets expectations" and avoid any problems.

But then the poor performers who are in denial about their bad performances are given license to think all is okay, even if they require ten times more management time than those who are doing well and pulling their weight.

I have heard more than one CEO say that he has never had a performance review. Just that proclamation commits the sin of avoidance. The truth is that leaders have a review every day; they know it, but they might just need that excuse so that they don't have to give reviews to their own people, or can say, "No one ever told me …"

The list of denial sins that lead to big fibs is long, but the biggest and most hurtful fib is when a CEO hides the performance of the company: It's when everything is portrayed as "up and to the right," when things are really flat or going down, or when the early warning signs of doom are taking hold, that denial and fibs start to surface.

Five Reasons Why CEOs Are Prone to Denial, Fibbing to Themselves—and Fudging for Others

1. **Failure to Set Realistic Priorities—Truth Avoidance**

   I want to play in the World Series and win an Academy Award, too, but it's not going to happen. Setting goals that are impossible to reach almost guarantees no one will try. "World's Leader," "Google Killer," "Dominant Player," and other such phrases give one pause to wonder exactly how the CEO plans to accomplish his plan, or raises the question, "What is he smoking?"

2. **Drowning in Detail and Bogging Down—Avoidance through Detail**

   Attention to details can be good, but not at the expense of leading or planning or selling or executing. Working on too much detail means the CEO is doing someone else's job. Worse, micromanagement is contagious and soon everyone will be redesigning expense report forms. Closure and the feeling of success occur when big and little projects are completed, not when details are further discussed.

3. **Spinning the Real Story—Avoiding the Truth**
   There is not much room for spinning stories when it comes to performance. When stuck, the CEO who says "we are doing great" rather than telling the truth is under the spell of the Devil. Without the truth, there is no hope that this the CEO will be effective.

4. **No Soul—Avoiding Yourself**
   Watch *Undercover Boss*: the leaders and CEOs that people want to follow are not afraid to disclose who they are and what's important to them. If the CEO talks only about his ski house and his kids at Yale, that's not soul. A leader that appears to be a listening, caring person, confident about making decisions, will create credibility.

5. **"What's In It for Me?" Is Never Clarified—Avoiding Sharing**
   Everyone believes the CEO gets big money no matter what happens. What's in it for him is clear, but what about everyone else? When no one knows what to do or how to do it or why they're doing it, the organization is stalled. The CEO has sinned by fudging the company's value for everyone else and may be stuck in yet another bog.

Avoiding Change: A Case of Waste

Verna has been buried in the bowels of one company for nearly thirty years and is about to retire. She is in a job no one has paid attention to for years and could easily spend her work days sucking down company-supplied sodas. But having been raised in a family with a strong work ethic, Verna is dedicated to doing her job, even though she's always known it has no purpose.

"Every week I collect a paycheck," Verna says, "and the company is about to support me in a comfortable retirement. I owe the company forty hours a week of the best job I am capable of doing." She is surrounded by beige-gray file cabinets filled with paper brought to her each day. It is Verna's task to make all those pieces of paper disappear, without actually destroying them. She has refined the system so that everything is logically filed and cross-filed and can be easily accessed upon request. Her one-woman operation is a model of efficiency.

She shows me a piece of paper with diagonal lines in the borders. On several of the lines are signatures. Each signature is from a management or support staff employee attesting that he or she has read and approved what's on the piece of paper. "Sometimes," Verna says, "a document will have as many as fifty signatures. My job is to make sure that each signature required is actually on the paper, and then to file the paper.

"I'm not sure why we go through this folderol. I used to ask, but no one had an answer except 'That's the way we do it.' I think maybe it was started long ago by an insecure executive who wanted to be sure if he made a bad decision it would be everyone's bad decision. Maybe it's a scare tactic to make people worry that if they make the wrong decision it will be on file forever. Or maybe they do it now, when they're always talking about employee involvement, to show that everything is a joint decision. Most likely we keep doing this stupid thing because everyone is afraid if they say anything about it they might look stupid."

Long ago, Verna tried to suggest ways in which her time could be put to better use. She knew when she went to her supervisor that by speaking up she could be putting an end to her own job. But she was willing to take the chance to stop the company from wasting its money and her time.

"No one wanted to hear about it. I've had job security all these years because it has been easier for them to avoid me and keep me doing a pointless task, than to admit it doesn't need to be done or take any responsibility for doing something about it."

It seems that no one has noted that a woman with exceptional organizational skills has been wasted for nearly thirty years, perhaps because no one other than the people who send her an endless succession of paper has ever stepped foot into her subterranean cubicle.

Verna envisions an exit interview in which she tells her current supervisor, or maybe even the manager of her department, how they have thrown away money instead of useless paper. "Not once," she says with ironic resignation, "in all the time I've been here, has anyone ever asked for a piece of paper I've filed."

WHY THE DIAMOND STAYS IN THE ROUGH

In fact, someone is aware of Verna's situation, even though there's not much chance of his changing it.

"I know she's being wasted," says Verna's current supervisor, Harry, who started with the company, in the mailroom, right after he graduated from high school. Harry, in his twenty years with the company, has always taken night classes to get a college degree and to acquire specific job-related skills. He knows what it is to be at the bottom of the corporate heap and try to dig out, to try to get past traditional obstacles, even though one has abilities that should be valued.

"It's hard to get the company to think of you in terms of anything other than what you're doing," Harry goes on to say. "I was halfway through my college courses and had completely revamped the mailroom and increased efficiency, by conservative measurement, at least 100 percent. I still had trouble getting anyone to think of me for anything other than the mailroom, where they did give me a slight promotion. And I did a lot of shouting—well, shouting for a corporate environment."

Harry continues: "Verna is a nice lady who doesn't want to cause a disturbance. When she did try to be heard, she got nowhere and gave up. If I'd been in this job sooner, I might have been able to help her, but now it's just too late. I have a limited head count. And to get a specific job changed would take an act of God, or worse, an act of Human Resources. If I try to upgrade her job and her responsibilities, I have to go through channels. I've made some discreet inquiries with people I know well and trust in HR. They say the same thing. If I try to do something, it's more likely that Verna's job will be eliminated. Some employee-hungry manager in another part of our department will grab the head count. Everyone is shorthanded, so there would be a feeding frenzy.

"They would probably offer Verna a package to just go away, but it would still make a difference to her retirement income. I'm trying to protect her, and I'll admit, work out a strategy so that when she does retire, I keep the head count. If I do anything else, she and I both lose. That's just the way things are. It's always been done his way, and it's going to take someone a lot more powerful than I am to change the system."

Case Lessons

- Pay special attention to employees who are willing to endanger their jobs to do the right thing.

- Don't keep doing the wrong thing just because it's always been done that way. Take a risk. Maybe if enough people are willing to tweak the system, it can be improved.

> Long-term stupidity isn't traditional; it's just long-term.

Fib Indicators

The Denial/Fibbing sin can be hard to detect because the difficult decisions are avoided and nothing much ever changes.

- **Work-Arounds Abound.** In spite of incompetent management, people in the trenches of any organization figure out how to get things done. If the conference rooms are always booked, they meet where they can. If the technology doesn't work, they use paper clips and duct tape to make it work. If there is a stream of well-known systems, processes, and just plain stuff (like the coffee pots) that don't work, then leaders are committing the sin of avoidance.

- **Picking Up a Hammer.** When there's an environment of "Here comes the boss, look busy," the lies and denial cannot be far behind. The boss surely knows that people are picking up that hammer to look busy. He is avoiding the fact that there are too many people or that no one knows what their job is or that people are not doing their job. In all cases, fibbing prevails.

- **Too Many Consultants**. Jokes about consultants are legion. Do you know one about consultants borrowing the watch to tell you the time? Rarely do consultants discover a problem or a way forward that is new to the organization. The issue is that these flaws have all been glossed over, and a consultant sheds light on them. The CEO of a dying company, who had no time for pleasant chit-chat, was the most denial-busting leader I met. The crisis created "fast truth." He once let me know, "I'm not going to pay a million dollars for you to tell us we are screwed up. Start there and tell me what you think we should do."

Consultants should be brought in to detect the truth and fix things, not to extend the sin of fudging.

- **Credenzaware.** A great name for all the strategies and plans and meaningless documents that pile up on the office furniture collecting dust. Even though teams spent hundreds of hours to complete the docs and the velo-bound presentations cost millions of dollars, they are never referred to. Nothing changes, nothing from the docs is implemented, and the sin of denial can be seen daily behind the leader's desk.

- **Deadwood Is Tolerated.** Every organization has deadwood—those people who, for whatever reason, stopped contributing long ago. Denying that deadwood exists is like letting the cancer grow.

Availability is Not a Skill

The great consulting firms are those that match skills of consultants with their client's needs. Unfortunately, many recruiters have become better at fudging than at matching skill sets. Which is to say, when people are available—"on the bench" or "on the beach"—they often miraculously take on the skills requested, and find themselves employed. Their "on the job training" may be carried out with lots of winks, nods, and completely billable time sheets.

 REDEMPTION

Picture the devil on one shoulder and an angel on the other. The devil is denial. Denial leads to fibbing. We know when we hear it and we know when we do it. Tackling the gnarly deals first will break the sin-of-fibbing trap. Worse, fibbing is both chronic and contagious. It can develop into a habit and can spread to those around you. There comes a split instant in any situation when you can avoid, deny, lie (and sin) or confront the issues head-on. Avoidance will almost always only delay, not solve. The sin will hang on you like an ill-fitting suit.

Talk to yourself if need be about how not to avoid the most important things that need to be done—personally and professionally.

Takeaways

- It's easier to remember what you say and think when you are vigilant about telling the truth always. One fib almost always leads to another, and the spiral of fibbing gets more complicated. To avoid the sin, don't fib at all and be brutally honest with yourself.

- Those things that make you wake up in the middle of the night and groan are the truths, decisions, activities, and people you are avoiding. A little confrontation will give you a better night's sleep. Direct is the way to be.

- What you most avoid in emails (those ones you gloss over, looking for something better) might be the decisions you most need to deal with now.

- Avoidance and fudging almost always makes the situation worse. Think of all those medical stories of the lump or the mole that was avoided for too long with an unhappy result.

- How do we know when we're being completely honest? Try writing in a journal that no one else sees. Compare what you write with how you deal with the situation. There should be congruity.

7

THE SIN: ARROGANCE

"Pursuing Other Interests"

It was a board meeting in a swanky hotel in New York City. The CEO had been doing a very good job and the company was enjoying success like never before. The board of directors was meeting the night before the official meeting began to discuss the CEO's performance and his compensation—a combination of base pay and stock options worth millions of dollars. Of course the CEO was not in the room. But while we were meeting to discuss his future and the likes of his country club membership, he was arrested in Manhattan for soliciting a prostitute. With consummate charm, he approached an undercover police officer for favors. Bail was posted to get him out of jail and very little was said. Nothing had to be said as everyone knew what had to happen. The crisis communications' experts were called in. Shortly thereafter, he was excised from the company in an announcement that alluded, ironically, to "his pursuing other interests."

It is too easy to pick on these guys—and there are many of them: John Edwards, Elliot Spitzer, Bill Clinton … and those are just a few of the politicians that we know of. And that's just about sex. What about business leaders who are less visible but are subject to the same sin of arrogance? We know they are not immune from temptation and the resulting rubble of careers and lives. We have seen too much to the contrary. We are talking about the sin that could be the original one: arrogance and the inherent belief that "I won't get caught," or, "Even if I do get caught, I can survive the trouble."

When a CEO commits the arrogance sin, the repercussions are endless and may ripple through an organization for years. People can lose their fortunes, as in the Bernie Madoff case. When the Enron team created their spot in business history, the retirements and careers of thousands went down the drain and the world began to look at corporate governance with a skeptical eye. The events surrounding the leadership changes at Hewlett Packard have rocked the perception of the great organization twice. Arrogance was at play in all of these cases. What makes the sin even more profound is the ultimate act of arrogance: all of these leaders thought that they wouldn't get caught.

Foolish Arrogance: I'm Sorry, I'm Not Here Right Now

A leader of a major well-known not-for-profit organization was having an affair with a young woman who worked for him. He thought it was secret, but everyone knew. Don't they always? Even though he ran a philanthropic enterprise that used technology extensively, he was not proficient with gadgets, especially when it came to all the options on the intercompany messaging system. Somehow, amazingly, he pushed the wrong buttons and confused the "message" feature with the "greeting" feature. He left what he thought was a message, but instead, recorded a greeting for all who called:"Hey, don't be mad at me. I know this isn't easy for you, and I will make it up to you. I promise I will leave my wife soon. We have the conference coming up, and we can spend a few days together in Hawaii in advance of that. Would you bring that pink thing I like so much? Just remember, I think about you in all these meetings I attend . . ."

Within an hour, the entire company had called his extension to hear his greeting. Ha Ha. One wonders who finally told him to listen to his own message. The CEO was gone within a year to be the CEO of a different but smaller not-for-profit. His paramour left long before he did in humiliation. People still talk about that greeting with wonder.

OFF-SITE ARROGANCE: VIVA LAS VEGAS

Early in my consulting career a wizened older partner (he was probably forty at the time) pulled me aside at an airport. We were flying to some exotic spot like Cincinnati for a meeting in full bore, three-piece suits. With a knowing look he lowered his voice and said, "Just remember, if you want to get ahead in this firm, what happens on the road stays on the road."

My imagination leapt to exotic places and fancy hotels with movie starlets sneaking around in the hallways looking for young, handsome consultants.

The story was repeated to me several times by partners, all married, all with a gleam in their eye, and my anticipation grew with every warning.

After twenty years on the road in consulting, I was still waiting for something to "happen." Nothing did. Maybe I was working too hard to look up and see what was happening around me. Maybe I was not good looking like the other partners. Maybe others thought I was gay, though that shouldn't have stopped something from happening. But nothing happened. I suspect now that nothing much happened to those other guys either.

On further consideration, the big takeaway here is that "things" just don't happen; a little work is involved. I didn't want something to happen so nothing did. Elliot Spitzer had to plan and think about how to try to transfer money so that it wouldn't show up on any statement. Even Mick Jagger in his prime had to make himself available if he wanted "satisfaction" and "heavy action." He had to "try."

~~~~~~

The-Hooker-on-Your-Arm Arrogance

At a trade show in Las Vegas the CEO of my client showed up with a hooker at what was supposed to be a working dinner. I guess she was working. She was charming and beautiful and although she didn't declare herself as an escort, she wasn't wearing a name tag with a convention label. I suppose prostitution is legal there, but there was no doubt in the minds of the twenty other people at dinner that the CEO's date didn't know a lot about computer disk drives. It was like a scene from the movie Leaving Las Vegas as he poured tequila down his throat and hers. He stayed with the company but was soon replaced as CEO.

~~~~~~

The one lesson we all learn in high school is that you will get caught. Go to the dance drunk—you will get caught. Marijuana seeds in a Petri dish in your closet—you will get caught. Stay out pass the curfew—you will get caught. Cut class because of a substitute teacher—you will get caught. Thomas Jefferson is still getting caught for indiscretions committed hundreds of years ago.

Most of us don't believe this lesson until, sure enough, we get caught. Yet CEOs seem to forget or ignore this one lesson I am sure they have learned. How is it that high profile, in-the-public-spotlight guys think that they won't get caught? On another level, how can they operate at the CEO level when they are obsessed with activities outside "planning and operations?" As one CEO told me, "You can't fight the battle on two fronts: at home and in the office."

This chapter is turning out to be about tasteless, inappropriate sex. It is really about arrogance. Or are the two sins the same thing for the sinful leader?

TEMPTATION

> "I live by one rule: No office romances, no way. Very messy, inappropriate … no. But, I live by another rule: Just do it … Nike."
> —Michael Scott, The Office

Admonitions abound about dating co-workers and sex in the workplace. Don't eat where you have bowel movements seems to be the standard, although what that phrase has to do with romance, exactly, escapes me. The meaning of the phrase goes into turbo-charge mode when it comes to dating anyone who reports to you. Since everyone reports to the CEO, it means everyone in the organization is off-limits—a rule that many seem to ignore because the temptation is just too great. And because they can get away with it for a while.

Perhaps beyond the physical temptation of sex is the temptation of "I will be the first one never to get caught." There is great competition to win that game, and it is as thrilling as any other aspect of "the chase." For a while it may even work … probably a shorter while than the cunning culprit may think. But alas, as we all know, everyone gets caught.

There is also the temptation of finding a sympathetic ear, a confidante, or a friend. As one CEO told me, "No one really understands how lonely it can be at the top, and she understands that part of me." The "she" in this case was a receptionist twenty years his junior.

A woman friend who claims to have the notches in her belt from affairs with any number of high-tech CEOs tells me that there is such a phenomenon as "sex radar." If the CEO is up for some fun, he sends off vibes that there is an opportunity for any willing takers. Part of the temptation is to see if there are any takers. There almost always are takers.

Social Networking Arrogance: Press CTRL-ALT-Delete

A pitch to venture capitalists (VCs) for funding is stressful. The VCs sit around the table, some paying attention, some on their Blackberries, while the entrepreneur tries to demonstrate that he/she has the idea for the next Google or Facebook. In the world of all new web applications, lots of the presentations have something to do with social networks or media. One CEO was preparing to show the PowerPoint presentation to the group and, as he was firing up his computer, his desktop screen was projected for all to see. Typically, no one pays attention during this phase of the warmup, but the background on the screen, the screen saver, was a photo of a naked woman— very naked. Now that he had everyone's attention, we looked at the icons, too. And there, wedged in between icons labeled "My Documents" and "Recycle Bin," were icons labeled "Porn" and "Teens." His request for millions of dollars was not granted.

Big Dick Arrogance: Just One Vote

In addition to handling all of his own sexual fantasies and his sex radar, most other sex issues and problems in the organization make their way to the CEO's desk. In a consulting assignment with a major trucking company, we were hosting focus groups with a cross-section of employees to get their perspectives on how to improve the company's performance. The meetings included management, members of the teamsters union, clerks—everyone we could find who might be willing to talk. Willingness to talk was never the problem.

One meeting was particularly stressful, for reasons unclear to me. But all the participants were exchanging sideways glances as if they were waiting for something to happen. Ten minutes into the meeting a very large, intimidating guy came in and slid his chair within two feet of where I was sitting. The silence was dramatic, but he broke it when he announced to the group, "Me and my big dick are both here."

One of the women in the room, also a teamster, replied, "You still only get one vote."

We were not there to vote, but that's what the teamsters were used to. Once the idea of voting was cancelled, they wanted to talk about the lack of leadership and common sense in the company. At the end of the meeting, the discussion returned to the large gentleman's initial comments, and by day's end three of the women had filed complaints with HR and the entire issue was on the desk of the CEO for him to decide how to handle it. The quote was part of the corporate legend, no matter how the CEO responsed. There were now union issues, sexual harassment issues, privacy issues, and too many consultant issues—to name just a few of the issues—and all were headed straight at the CEO. He looked out of his window at a crew from the local utility; they were digging a ditch and chatting it up with each other.

He said, "I wish I had a job like that," and at that moment he meant it.

CONFIDENCE VS. ARROGANCE

Economic turmoil has taught all leaders how to cut costs within the organization. Granted, some do it better than others, but through the bitter pill of experience, everyone knows how to do it. The implementation of cost cutting says much about a leader and can define the difference between confidence and arrogance.

Steve was a leader who had a good sense of his bank and a good sense of the market but was watching the bank's earnings slowly spiral downward and lose a position in the market. He sensed a need to just start cutting costs and he knew that the cost structure would not budge an inch without cutting people. "Cutting costs is not about the free coffee or travel," he would repeat over and over, "cutting costs is all about cutting people." The analysis began and the lists of people were compiled. But before the cost cuts were "executed," Steve made a pronouncement. He said, "I am confident we have the right number of people. I just think they are doing the wrong things." And with that simple statement, a plan was set in place and thousands of people re-focused on customer service and revenue and the performance of the bank changed for the better. In describing the turnaround, Steve gave full credit to the people and led others to believe he had very little to do with it. The bank's success was based on the people's willingness to change. He was confident and inspired confidence from those people.

By contrast, Phil, the leader of a big tech company that was struggling with the integration of a large acquisition, was stumped. The acquisition was risky and its success or failure would dictate the career success of the CEO. He pushed and threatened and although the deal was done, the company that was being acquired pushed back. They didn't want to be a part of the bigger entity. Other senior managers on both sides got together and formed a large set of teams to figure out how best to do the integration. It worked. The integration was flawless, people kept their jobs and the stock price went up. In announcing the miracle of the flawless integration, he boasted of the simplicity of the process and how he led it. He predicted more great teamwork to follow. The results didn't follow because the group was demoralized by an arrogant leader who took all the credit.

SHARING THE BLAME FOR ARROGANCE

There is no escape for the CEO and he should know that when he takes the job. When a bunch of athletes are arrested for sexual misconduct, the assumption is that the coach runs a lax ship where bad behavior is tolerated. There is no shortage of examples in that regard. When there is misconduct of any kind in an organization the assumption is that the CEO runs a ship where rules are bent, whether or not that is true. There are so many examples of accounting fraud, poisoned peanuts, and lying and stealing in general that sexual misconduct has moved down the list of things that make us wonder about the judgment of CEOs. When one steals billions, how exciting can a night in a motel with a hooker be? All sex activity that the CEO needs to get involved in, directly or indirectly, is still plenty interesting but is often swept under any rug to be found.

The on-campus recruiting dance is a senior year ritual for college students and the lifeblood of big organizations that rely on annual infusions of new people that they can force to travel, or go through training that is more like hazing. So it was that representatives from a major consumer products company visited a Midwestern college in search of marketing and sales trainees. The interview schedules were filled with marketing majors but the Director of Sales wanted to try an experiment and interview graphic art majors. He explained, "We need more creativity around here."

It just so happens that a very large percentage of graphic art majors are women and his interview schedule was 100% women. After an uneventful interview day the company invited several of the students back for second interviews at headquarters. A few of the graphic art students were individually invited to a downtown hotel for their second interview. Each of them really wanted a job. Each had a separate time slot so no one student ever saw the others and while at the hotel, each was asked to put on a pair of panty hose (the company made them) and then was subjected to a wrestling match with the interviewer that he explained was a test to see how they could handle stress.

One of the students was a daughter of the CEO of a Fortune 50 company. When he learned of the "interview" he called the President of the University. The President of the University called the CEO of the recruiting company in question. Turns out the "interviewer," the Director of Sales, had been fired between the on-campus interview and the incident in the hotel. No one could find the guy.

I sat in the room and watched two CEOs and the President of a university rub the bridge of their noses while shaking their heads while one muttered, "The god-damnedest things I have to spend my time on." It was a mess that took lots of time, energy and money to resolve.

Finally there was justice as the recruiter was found, charged with assault, and served time.

ARROGANCE INDICATORS

Your CEO may suffer from arrogance if he demonstrates some of the following traits:

- **Ignores Facts.** In the face of cold analytical data, the CEO who claims to "know better" is sure to sin. Sometimes pattern recognition and intuition does help in decision-making, but disregarding analysis is a sure way to create problems.

- **Believes in Superheroes.** "They can't fire me!" is a phrase I've heard more than once from a CEO. Those who say it will probably be fired sooner than later. Superman was not a CEO: When not in costume, he was a humble reporter.

- **Discusses SAT Scores.** To get to the top, most leaders are pretty smart. Most have distinguished academic credentials. That stellar academic performance is not indicative of performance as a leader is a fact that everyone knows, so flaunting those credentials is arrogant.

- **Ears Are Plugged.** You won't see any blockage in the ears so the signals for plugged ears are not easy to spot. Telltale signs are the constant "Uh huh" or the glancing around to see if there is something better going on nearby. To not be a good listener is to commit the sin of arrogance every day. All day.

 # REDEMPTION

Any CEO who cannot keep his pants on is en route to a life of sin. So a simple rule to avoid that fate would be to keep one's pants on at all times. The problem is not about trousers. The problem is the arrogance of the CEO.

Any CEO has a healthy ego or he wouldn't have moved through the world to get to that lofty spot. An ego is a good thing until it is dominated by the arrogant part of the formula. While I suspect that I can provide advice about resurrection, CEOs and other leaders seem to have a blind spot when it comes to the arrogance gene. Why couldn't the politicians that followed his example learn from Bill Clinton? Why couldn't John Edwards learn from Elliot Spitzer? Why couldn't Bernie Madoff learn from Kenneth Lay? Why didn't Anthony Weiner learn from any of them? The answer is their sheer arrogance and the even more despicable trait of hubris. Hubris is when you are so proud and arrogant that you know it will lead to your downfall, but you indulge in it anyway.

Advice given about inappropriate behavior in the workplace, especially about arrogance and sex, has been largely ignored since time began, but there does seem to be hope for change. Call it better living at work through technology. That is, every device in our pockets has a video recorder and digital camera on it. Problem behaviors can be posted on the web in a matter of seconds. Catching someone in the act—and getting caught—has never been easier.

Takeaways

Some leaders seem hellbent on getting into hell via arrogance. For the rest of us, the following advice is rendered with the hopes of our foregoing hell:

- Getting caught often means losing your job. No matter the crime—if you're worried about getting caught, don't do it.

- Arrogance is measured in daily slights and boorish behavior, not in grand demonstrations of hubris. Look for the small things you do every day that send out signals of arrogance.

- If all your friends at work are arrogant, chances are, you are too. Find new friends if you still can.

- Don't confuse arrogance with the confidence to set goals and succeed. It might be a thin line, but here's the litmus test: The leader who sets aggressive goals and shares the credit for all the successes is confident. The leader who takes all the credit is arrogant.

8

THE SIN: VANITY

"Did You Read My Book?"

There are rock-star quality CEOs. Steve Jobs, Jack Welch, Larry Ellison, Oprah Winfrey, Barack Obama, Indra Noovi from Pepsi, to name a few. Books are written about them. They write books, give speeches, get invited to the White House to opine on what is ailing the economy, have their little ink portraits in the *Wall Street Journal* and make lots of money. On the positive side, a rock-star CEO can position the company as a well-managed, hip organization just by virtue of having him there. Organizations are appraised through their leaders. On the down side, when do they manage the company if they are busy writing books and dining and opining in the White House? When it's all about them, it can't always be about the company.

You Probably Thought That Song Was About You

The Telco CEO prided himself on the thoroughness with which he conducted performance reviews. He kept meticulous notes during the course of the year, and when your time for a review was due, you had his undivided attention for a good hour. Upon entering his office, he would declare, "I'm yours for the next hour!"

All those who reported to him would rather have spent that hour getting a root canal.

The stories about each review he conducted were the same. He would open the review with something like, "You know you've done a very good job this year. I'd like to spend some time focusing on the areas that need improvement," and then he would blast each of his direct reports for fifteen minutes until he'd say, "Let me tell you about my career…" And then would describe his storied past at McKinsey and IBM.

Although he gave everyone the highest possible rating and a big raise at the end of the review, what everyone heard was that he or she was a screw-up … and that the CEO was living on his past laurels and he couldn't wait to talk about them, like a forty-year-old who talks about his high school football heroics.

MUSHROOM MANAGEMENT: MUSHROOMS CAN BE MOLDY!

"These employee suggestion boxes and newsletters are a bunch of crap. The suggestions go directly to trash and the newsletters are about softball scores. The CEO here practices 'mushroom management.' We are like mushrooms: he keeps us in the dark and feeds us bullshit."

—A quote taken from an employee suggestion system

The Telco boss had turned what should have been a clear moment of his employees' accomplishments into a nebulous defeat through the sin of vanity. It is hard to be around truly vain people. For the rock star-type CEO, it is always about him, no matter what "it" is. The leader who is under the spell of the vanity sin believes that the organization, no matter the size, will fail without him.

Executive vanity can be subtle. It may not show itself in hairstyles and cars. It may show itself in being dismissive and nonresponsive. Vanity may show itself in the form of "I know what I'm doing; 'they' don't need to know."

HOW WE CREATE "ROCK-STAR CEOs"

In his famous "Speech to the Graduates" essay of 1980, Woody Allen announced:

> *More than at any other time in history, mankind faces a crossroads. One path leads to despair and utter hopelessness. The other, to total extinction. Let us pray we have the wisdom to choose correctly. I speak, by the way, not with any sense of futility, but with a panicky conviction of the absolute meaninglessness of existence that could easily be misinterpreted as pessimism. It is not. It is merely a healthy concern for the predicament of modern man.*

The CEO often feels like he is faced with the same tortured crossroads. Reduce costs? Reduce prices? Shut down offices? Move jobs offshore? He can hardly rise above these complicated and no-win situations like an air balloon and yet, he can't become "one of the people." In so many ways the organization itself elevates its CEO to the status of Emperor, expecting him to "do right by them," and make sound, effective decisions from the "lonely at the top" perspective.

Even though some would say there is mounting evidence to the contrary, I repeat my conviction that most CEOs are trying to do the right thing. How each of us defines "the right thing" is different. For some, it could be a multi-million dollar birthday bash at the company's expense. Or maybe the right thing means never taking bailout money from the government and then paying out millions of dollars to executives in bonuses.

When downsizing occurs or when there seems to be a string of bad news, someone somewhere, a leader, a CEO, is acting on what he believes to be the right thing. Hopefully, the right thing will be based on data. But we paint traps for leaders, often without knowing it. We cast them as heros, capable of solving ponderous problems. We elect officials who campaign on change platforms. But as soon as change happens, we scream, "No, not that!" The CEO is looking at the Woody Allen crossroads again.

And so, evangelism must become part of the leader's personality. Think Howard Schultz at Starbucks. Think Herb Kelleher at Southwest Airlines. Even quiet CEOs have an evangelist gene that comes into play when needed. But that passion and evangelism can't go to the point where the vanity of the leader takes the organization over the proverbial cliff. "We can do it!" doesn't work when the vainglorious CEO is taking the organization down the drain. Optimism is required—if the leader doesn't "believe," who will? But the combination of vanity and optimism can lead to a den of sin. Think John Edwards.

Although we all want to believe the evangelist and retain our own optimism, a realistic perspective is always necessary. A healthy perspective recognizes the good and the possible while being honest about the reality of the situation. Consider these important points:

- Sometimes things **are** better than they seem. Even though our trust may have been violated many times by leaders, we can't afford to be completely cynical about leadership.

- Who would you rather work with—pessimists or optimists? Either trait is contagious.

- Sometimes doing the right things is not popular. But the CEO who can do the unpopular right things and maintain the optimism of the organization should be applauded.

TEMPTATION

The rhetorical question "If you could be reborn as anyone, who would it be?" is making the rounds again. A lot of the people I know are answering the question by saying, "My kids." The implication is that the kids are pampered, fool around on Facebook all day, are waited on by someone who gets them drinks, drives them around, does the hard homework for them, and so on. It is a good life, and many CEOs lead that same life of adolescent pampering. It is no wonder some of them behave like adolescents. They can act like adolescents, so they do.

Rock star-leaders often have a taste for the better life and develop expensive habits that can make the rest of the organization seethe and get the leader in trouble. But the vanity temptation is very sensuous and can pull any of us into its spell. Early in my career I had a staff job at a major oil company. My boss there never did anything, and slyly took all the credit based on other's work. It was not an easy work environment for me, so after a job hunt landed me a better job, I smugly went to him to announce my resignation.

I spoke out of turn when I declared, "I don't know how all the work will get done now." I was vain about my contribution and just knew that the department would fall apart when I left.

He had heard this before, obviously, and handed me this poem, already printed. It was the only thing that boss taught me, and I've kept the poem as a reminder of the vanity sin.

There Is No Indispensable Man
by Saxon N. White Kessinger, 1959

Sometime when you're feeling important;
Sometime when your ego's in bloom
Sometime when you take it for granted
You're the best qualified in the room,

Sometime when you feel that your going
Would leave an unfillable hole,
Just follow these simple instructions
And see how they humble your soul;

Take a bucket and fill it with water,
Put your hand in it up to the wrist,
Pull it out and the hole that's remaining
Is a measure of how you'll be missed.

You can splash all you wish when you enter,
You may stir up the water galore,
But stop and you'll find that in no time
It looks quite the same as before.

The moral of this quaint example
Is do just the best that you can,
Be proud of yourself but remember,
There's no indispensable man. (Or woman).

CEO as Royalty

Emperors also enjoy the hierarchy surrounding them. An emperor needs dukes and lords and princes and jesters, to name a few, that make him seem important. A CEO emperor needs organization charts. The org charts that are developed in the name of illustrating who is on top are outdated as soon as they are developed, but it doesn't matter as long as the same name is on the top. Predictions of the death of the hierarchical organization have been exaggerated because emperors like hierarchy. Former Marine officers are especially aware of the command and control inherent in the hierarchy emperors delight in.

Org charts are usually in the shape of a pyramid, but the only thing they might show clearly is who's on top. A big reorganization at a major aerospace company produced the same old horses, same old glue. Matrix management means no one knows who his boss is.

"Calling Number 43"

"A vice president from London called to tell me he was my new boss. I told him to take a number and get in line." So says a manager at a consulting firm

VANITY AND COMPENSATION

Executive pay and the concept of CEO vanity are often linked. Does anyone really deserve to make $60 million a year? Probably not. Especially if the company is not doing well. Steve Jobs takes a salary of $1.00 a year and is not accused of vanity. We all agree: if someone offered us a big salary, we would take it. But the price that comes with it is the perception that you think you are worth that much.

And, the more at odds such luxury is with the organization, the more of a sin it becomes. The recent line of CEOs at Wal-Mart have been successful because they have not given in to the sin of vanity. Stockholders and employees demand that the leader of the corporation that describes its mission as "saving people money so they can live better" be someone who lives that premise. For the CEO of Wal-Mart to carry something like Louis Vuitton luggage would be a concession to vanity. Conversely, the CEO of Louis Vuitton may give in a little to vanity because that's what consumers want in that brand. A Louis Vuitton purchase is a vanity purchase.

VANITY INDICATORS

A CEO may be considered vain if he evidences one or more of the following traits:

- **Believes the PR.** CEOs can be PR machines, but that carefully crafted image may or may not be true. Leaders can be honored for serving the community, for serving on boards, and all the other activities that the trappings of power bring. In the middle of the accolades, the more humbly the CEO receives his recognition and the more he shares it, the less likely is vanity infecting him.

- **Surrounds himself with suck-ups.** A true leader will include people around him who will challenge and disagree with him, when appropriate. A vain leader will surround himself with those who cover for him, always say yes, and play politics.

- **Engages in pseudophilanthropy.** There are CEOs who give away corporate money, but lead people to believe the money is coming out of their own pocket. Major accolades to Bill and Melinda Gates and Warren Buffett for calling on CEOs to give. Just don't make it yet another vanity play.

- **Calls too many meetings.** A CEO can call for a meeting any time of the day or night or weekend and demand that all attend and be prepared so he can listen. When the meetings are only called to feed the CEO's need to be important, the sin of vanity is in full force.

- **Uses airplanes, clubs, and drivers.** The cost/benefit of a corporate jet rarely pencils out and is always seen as a luxury. So, too, are many of the other trappings of being a CEO. There are times when the perks are warranted for sales and growth. But when perks are merely flaunted or indulged, the vanity flames are often being fanned.

- **Is absent with no excuse.** The CEO who doesn't show up when he says he will or is always late might be suffering from the unforgivable sin (for a CEO) of being disorganized. But more likely, he is hitting the vanity button.

 REDEMPTION

It is too simple to say that the cure for the vanity sin is to kill the book tour, or to simply "stop being vain." Vanity is much more nuanced than that and requires both a self-aware leader and one who can gauge how he is playing in the organization.

More than anything, killing vanity will involve asking people to tell you the truth. In other words, walk that mile in another's shoes. The television show *Undercover Boss* is wildly popular because it features CEOs not being vain, but being willing to see their corporate culture as their workers may see it. Every worker in the world enjoys that show of humanity.

For the CEO who wants to write: make your book about others, not yourself.

The real leadership double whammy happens when heaps of vanity accompany poor results. Work from "the results" backward, and let others bestow the praise.

Takeaways

- Leadership vanity involves managing a complex set of paradoxes. A leader is always in charge, a condition that requires him to believe he's in charge. Yet, it's like balancing being "the man" without being "the man." Employees want their leader to be on the covers of *Fortune* and *Forbes,* but they also want the leader to be humble.

- Vanity in a leader is not about mirrors and appearance. It is more about hyping his own infallibility, and his lack of willingness to listen to anyone else.

- Remember that nobody is indispensable.

- Watch how teenagers act, particularly how they entitle themselves to luxuries and indulgences. Don't do it.

9

THE SIN: BEING AN ASSHOLE

Pecked To Death

Some will say this should be the longest chapter in the book. It may be considered the ultimate summation of the preceding ones. For example ... The CEO of a big technology company was holding court at an all-employee meeting in the auditorium of the local community college. Every local employee trudged to the theater where the night before The American Idol Live! tour had played. All employee meetings always remind me of grammar school fire drills—a lot of people standing around waiting for the all-clear signal.

For those who couldn't be there in person, including several thousand employees in India and China, there were satellite downlinks. Everyone was trying to figure out what time of day or night it was outside of the U.S. and feeling sorry for those who were up in the middle of the night for the extravaganza. At the main event stage, major sound and video engineering was in place and PR people were everywhere. The corporate events staff people were wearing matching golf shirts and headphones. The purpose of the big folderol was to announce the company's new products.

As the lights went on and the cameras started rolling, the CEO strode on to the stage, wearing an expensive black T-shirt and with a big smile on his face. He proclaimed:

> *"Welcome to all—all over the world. Thanks for being here and for making this the best place in the world to work. In fact, one of my goals is to get on the list of the Best Places to Work in America. I think we can do it because of all of you, our employees, are our most important asset.*
>
> *"We are here to launch our new products. But before I start describing our fabulous new offerings, I want to talk to you about our corporate culture. Everyone keeps yelling at me about it and telling me how important it is that I set the corporate culture and that it comes from me, the CEO. So today I want to help you understand how I look*

at culture here. My thoughts were formed by a story I learned recently on the Discovery Channel."

Red Flag One (with murmurs from the audience): Our CEO watches the Discovery Channel? Is he thinking about buying the channel? Is he spending quality time with his family? Could this be a good thing?

Watching the Discovery Channel could be a good thing for our CEO, many thought. This could be a side of him we don't know about. Maybe he has lots of kittens at home. Before any questions about the Discovery Channel could be entertained, the CEO continued: "On that show I learned a fascinating metaphor that applies to our corporate culture. Did you know that in the elephant world, if an elephant is injured, the rest of the herd will gather very close around the sick one? The herd will protect it from predators and nurse its wounds until it is healthy again. They will stay with the sick elephant for weeks on end and never leave its side until it can fend for itself. It's a very touching story."

His eyes were wide as he said, "I learned about the culture of the penguin world, too, on the Discovery Channel. In the penguin world if one becomes sick, the other penguins will gather around it and peck it to death. Then they eat it."

Finally, he exalted, "I want our culture to be like the penguin world!"

Red Flag Two: When the CEO makes a big pronouncement to stunned silence, it is never good. And when the wrong lesson is gleaned from the Discovery Channel, how does he interpret other data?

After the stunned silence broke, the CEOs executive staff chuckled and applauded while the rest of the company shook their heads in disbelief and looked at each other, not sure if he was serious or not. When they finally realized that he was serious, they could not understand what they did to deserve such an asshole running the company.

I'M AN ASSHOLE BECAUSE I CAN BE

Let me repeat that while most CEOs are not in the asshole category, too many are. And, when pressed, many a CEO will admit that there were days when, against his better judgment, he acted like an asshole and felt bad about it because he knew he was on his way to hell. But he'll claim he couldn't help it.

Some CEOs take great pleasure in being an asshole. In *The No Asshole*

Rule, Bob Sutton draws our attention to asshole behavior. I fear that the culprits aren't reading that book. I fear that the culprits don't read. I tend to doubt they write.

Asshole tendencies can flare up in all of us. Admit it, you have been there. But the difference between a real asshole and someone who is an asshole only on rare occasions is the latter's ability to feel remorse. On those few occasions where I acted like a butthead I was overwhelmed with guilt. Once, while in a terrible hurry, I gave an elderly driver the middle finger for driving slow and blocking an intersection. When I made the gesture I couldn't see who was driving, but there was no doubt by the sad look in his eye that he saw me and my rude behavior. I was so overwhelmed with guilt that I followed him until he pulled into his driveway so that I could apologize. Of course, by then he didn't know what I was talking about and thought I was a stalker, but I felt better. Or, at least like less of an asshole.

ASSHOLISM: WHAT GOES AROUND ...

There are conflicting sentiments as to whether or not assholes will get their comeuppance in the end. I am never sure if that means that they will someday meet their match and get treated as poorly as they have treated others; or if it means they will burn in hell for being an asshole. References to "his bad karma" and "he can't be happy" are usually a part of this conversation. I believe both will happen. The asshole will get thrown in jail, or his wife will leave him, or his children will hate him, or the board will fire him; plus he will burn in hell. The asshole is no doubt oblivious to this conversation because he probably doesn't think he is one. If he did know he was one would he change? Maybe not.

A growing software company was having problems with profitability. The company was always just a little short on the revenue line. The CEO was certain that people weren't busy enough trying to "find the money." The "people" to whom he referred was not a small group; this was a company with nearly five thousand employees. In a private meeting with me the CEO pulled out a manila folder with many pages of a printed spreadsheet in it. He tapped the folder and said, "See this? This is our problem." I wondered if there were too many spreadsheets in the company or too many manila folders but didn't say anything.

"People are our problem," he continued, "and I am going to fix it without a lot of bullshit business school processes. Instead, you are going to fix it for me just using this one little file." He opened the file and I could now see that every employee in the company was listed on the spreadsheets. "What I want you to do is go down the list and make a simple note next to each name on the list," and he handed me two pens—one red, one black. "Make a note next to every name: either a black R for revenue generator or a red NR for non-revenue generator."

I knew the NRs would include basically everyone in any type of a staff role, like finance, legal, and human resources, and I knew where the conversation was headed. He finished the conference by saying, "When you finish with the NRs, cut half of them out of the company. It's that simple."

Eventually there were major staff cuts in that software company, and it was clear forever after to everyone inside and out that non-revenue generators were not valued. People in functions like human resources and accounting were hiding. At least people knew that if they were in a non-revenue generating staff role that the asshole would be after them. In fact, the CEO knew he was perceived as Ivan the Terrible and it didn't faze him one way or the other. He would disregard any comments about morale with remarks like, "If they want a cappuccino machine they should go work at Google."

The problem became they did go to work at Google. Those staff people in finance and human resources and marketing left the company in droves and the problems escalated. If you want to have a disenchanted workforce, screw up their pay and benefits. Eventually, the leader reconciled his stance with a more balanced approach.

One doesn't have to be the CEO to be an asshole; it can happen at any and all levels and can lead to the fires of hell. If you think you are an asshole, you probably are one. If you claim you don't know one, you probably are one too. Here are a few signals, and if the shoe fits …

TEN EARLY SIGNS THAT YOUR BOSS IS AN ASSHOLE
(OR THAT YOU ARE ONE)

- The boss who can often be heard saying, "Your job is to make me look good" probably needs help to look good. Never make him look too good.

- Being prone to outbursts that lead to unintentional spitting, and to everyone else laughing hilariously behind the scenes.

- Someone else leaves Robert Sutton's book *The No Asshole Rule* on his chair at night.

- He never, ever gives anyone a good review and constantly refers to his time at GE, IBM, or some other previous employer that he holds up as a paragon of management.

- Doesn't take the time to know anyone's name other than his boss's spouse.

- Tells crude racist, sexist, homophobic jokes, even subtly.

- Intimidates people into not taking vacations or time off, but always does it himself.

- Makes his assistant take care of his kids on "Take Your Kids to Work Day."

- Rolls his eyes, clicks his tongue, winks at others whenever someone makes a suggestion.

- Is always, always, always late or cancels at the last minute.

THE MORALE PROBLEM FOR THE ASSHOLE

The subject of morale is one that puzzles many CEOs. They are not sure what to do about it, or if they should care about it. Those worth their salt usually do. If morale is poor, many CEOs attribute the pall over people to low salaries. If morale is good, the same CEO is not sure why people are happy, but pleased that it is so. He may attribute the happy morale situation to strong leadership. In either case, rationalization is sure to follow.

In a company where morale was in the dumpster, I heard a CEO proclaim, "Morale may be bad, but the company is on the right track. Hey, those guys who were rowing the Viking boats were never happy, but those boats got there fast and allowed everyone time to pillage and plunder!"

In response to excellent morale, I heard another CEO proclaim that it was due to enhancements in the employee benefits package. The importance of benefits should not be underplayed. But I doubt they had an impact on morale, and I wondered about the CEO's awareness of what was happening in the company. Morale is affected most by the tone of a company's direction and leadership, and by the staff appreciating its own contribution. Morale pertains to job security and satisfaction. All of these critical morale factors are in the hands of the CEO. But the asshole on his way to hell doesn't care about morale.

BOWLING SCORES AND CAFETERIA MENUS?—NOT!

The CEO of USAir conducted an all-employee survey during one of the many times the company has been in trouble. The results were devastating in evaluating both the leadership and the airline as a work environment. The key finding of the results was employees felt communications were very poor and they needed to hear how the airline was doing on a regular basis. To his credit, the CEO ordered an immediate change in how the company communicated to all employees and launched a daily newsletter. The content was material that people cared about. Instead of bowling scores and blood drives, the newsletter contained material about weather, passenger count, and maintenance—all the things that employees of an airline care about—and an email copy was sent to all employees. For those who were harder to email, a hard copy was available every single day.

In a follow-up survey, the employees were asked the same set of questions and the biggest issue of the company was identified as … "communications." Rather than proclaiming the employees stupid and asking, "Do they want a newsletter every hour?" the CEO said, "I think communications is not the issue. Let's see what we are really trying to fix." He did further assessments and found that the people didn't like the new way and didn't understand why they were moving away from what made them great. So the company re-focused on its core strengths and it moved forward toward profitability. The CEO moved away from hell.

HOW MANY KINDS OF ASSHOLES ARE THERE?

The Asshole CEO can take two forms: active or passive-aggressive. The active one is the "imperial" kind we hear so much about. The kind who yells, berates, criticizes, and generally has people frightened for their job and well-being all the time. The passive-aggressive type of asshole CEO can be just as pernicious and is probably more widespread. He's the guy who throws around the side comments, directs a critical glance at the wrong time, or rolls his eyes as someone else is speaking. The passive-aggressive CEO, who uses nuance and subtleties to erode others' confidence, is the one who knowingly destroys people and their careers, and he can be even more hurtful than the what-you-see-is-what-you-get monster.

TEMPTATION

I recently heard an interesting exchange between a CEO's Executive Assistant and a subordinate who was trying to speak to him so that a decision could be made.

Subordinate: "Hey, I have been calling (Mr. CEO) for days. Is there a reason he won't take my calls?"

EA: "(Mr. CEO) doesn't take calls, he makes calls."

Subordinate: "But this is about the meeting coming up. Why won't he return calls?

EA: "Because he doesn't have to."

The exchange reminded me of the time I flew from San Francisco to Newark, NJ, on a red-eye flight to meet with a CEO at his request. The meeting with him was the only reason I was taking the trip. After flying all night, sleeping very little, and taking a "shower" in the sink at Newark Airport, I arrived at his office via taxi, all decked out for our 9:00 am meeting. When I arrived, his EA looked me up and down and informed me that, "Mr. CEO called in sick this morning."

I was stunned and recounted in an instant how much the flight cost, physically and financially. After a sigh, my only response to the EA was the rhetorical question, "Who did he call?" As in, who approved his not being there because he is sick, or who does the U.S. President call when he is calling in sick and won't show up for the day's work?

These two stories exemplify the asshole temptations to which any CEO may succumb. It's almost like a spell: the intensity of the job propels the CEO to consider only results, appearances, and the power of his position. This is the classical Machiavellian proposition wherein the means justify the ends. It's a natural outgrowth of "Because I Can."

When this temptation takes over, "thinking twice" goes out the window. Any thoughtful CEO is not considered an asshole and will miss the direct chute into hell. Does the word thoughtful come into mind with names like Jeffrey Skillings of Enron, Bernie Madoff, or Elliot Spitzer? Maybe they've had occasion to become thoughtful. But when they were under the asshole spell, I doubt it.

Tune in to CNBC, Fox Business, CNN, or any program that has a constant parade of CEOs going through, and you can almost pick out the assholes based on the degree of thought with which any one of them considers a question. There's no exact science to this perspective, but I bet we could all come close to pegging any CEO on the "Asshole Meter" based on a five-minute TV interview.

GIVING AT THE OFFICE

In survey after survey when people are asked about the traits they most admire in a leader, the traits that are often cited include integrity, taking a long-term view, strong decision making and fairness with people. Another word that has crept into many of the surveys is "stewardship," and it is one that I like. A variation of the word stewardship, and one that is always high on my list of admirable traits, is generosity. A true asshole CEO will be known instantly by his lack of generosity.

Generosity as a CEO means different things to different people, but here are a few examples of generous and non-generous behaviors:

- **Let them eat cake.** The CEO of a Standard & Poor's 500 company averaged $10.4 million in total pay in 2008. The outliers in either direction get most of the attention, but nearly a million dollars a month is pretty good pay. A "generous" CEO will not abuse the privilege of executive pay, and will even share the glory a bit. How much is enough for the CEO, compared to the rest of the company? Lots of websites are keeping track of CEO pay. Most do it with an eye toward the egregious nature of the compensation and how it compares to the people who are doing "real" work. Some accounts are kept by labor unions like the AFLCIO. The lists of who are sinners are not hard to find.

- **Let a little light shine.** The CEO does not have to be the bride at every wedding and the corpse at every funeral. Sharing the stage and the limelight with others is another way to be generous. When Al Gore suggested he "invented the Internet," in spite of his nontechnical background, it raised some credibility questions. Employees know that a CEO may not do "real" work, so if he takes credit instead of giving credit, everyone will know. Giving away all the credit is a good way to stay to stay out of the asshole box.

- **Pass it on.** A generous CEO wants to be remembered as someone who built something that endured, like Bill Hewlett and David Packard. An asshole will take all that he can while he is in the CEO seat and not worry about what happens when he is gone—like Hank Greenberg at AIG, in my opinion.

TOTAL ASSHOLISM: DODGING SNIPERS

It was a huge sales presentation, maybe a presentation that could "make" the company. The CEO of the selling company was presenting to the CEO and executive team of the buying company.

No matter how much planning is involved, it is true with 100 percent of presentations that someone will be at Kinko's at 2:00 am making copies and binding them. It is almost always the youngest man or woman on the travelling dog-and-pony-show team. In this case, it was two young women at a Kinko's in a big urban setting, and as they were leaving the shop at 2:00 am they heard shots from somewhere above and dove under a van parked on the street. It took them only a minute—and some police on bullhorns—to learn that they, along with everyone else in the vicinity, were pinned down by a sniper.

They stayed quiet for a moment and then called the CEO on a cell phone. He was sleeping in preparation for the 8:00 am presentation. From his hotel room the CEO heard the story from the young women still under the van. He asked, "Do you have the finished presentations?" They said yes. He responded, "Then make a run for it."

They did and they survived.

GENES VS. ENVIRONMENT

Smart people have raised the question, "Does the CEO job make him an asshole, or is it a style and temperament that he brings to the job?" My response is always, "Does it matter?" I do think that if there is a proclivity to go in that direction, the CEO role will tip the balance in a bad way. A person with a family background of alcoholism may face the demons most effectively if he works in a tavern. Others who might go to that dark side should instead know their own weaknesses and be on guard. Regarding assholes, you know who you are because the chances are good if you have that gene that you've been called an asshole once or twice before.

Most CEOs who are assholes didn't become one just as they reached the pinnacle of the organization. Chances are that behavior helped them get into that office, and now there is no reason to change. Some of us have seen that and said to ourselves, "Hey, if I want to be a CEO, maybe I need to act that way too."

 REDEMPTION

Some assholes are so far gone that we are more interested in putting them on the fast track to hell than we are in their redemption. Rather than trying to fix an impossible situation, our interest is in expediting the CEO to hell through murder or by outsourcing the action to hit men. Assholes transform only through a look in the mirror, as Michael Jackson would have said. The change requires self-awareness; the lack thereof is exactly what creates the asshole to begin with. Nonetheless, these few redemptive scenarios might block the path to hell for the CEO:

- Give your money to worthy causes. It is a sure way to redemption. When was the last time you heard someone call Bill Gates an asshole?

- Set up a timetable for when you will leave the organization. If you are an asshole and can't help it, your departure will give people something to look forward to.

- Take a lot of time off, away from the office, and give responsibility to someone who is not an asshole.

- Talk and listen to the people who are doing real work. Learn the words "on the street," and factor it into executive decisions.

- Surround yourself with people who will tell you when you are acting like an asshole. A spouse is usually good at this.

Any CEO might get away with the sins of cowardice or inactivity for a while. The sin of being an asshole will be revealed much more quickly, no matter what level you are in the organization. This role is easy to get into and very difficult to get out of, and it can dictate the arc of a career. The first time you hear the word whispered, take stock of your own actions and change before your soul goes into the abyss. There will always be the CEO who proudly but inadvertently proclaims himself to be an asshole, like the guy who talked about elephants and penguins. For them, there may be no redemption, and we just might have to relish the fact that no one likes them and that they will always be known as "that asshole."

Takeaways

I always wonder when I see asshole behavior whether the perpetrator knows how he is acting. Sometimes I suppose it is easier to be an asshole than it is to not be one; being an asshole might be camouflage for the path of least resistance. Always choose not to be one. You can learn how not to be an asshole just as easily as you can learn to be one.

- The late Studs Terkel, the great chronicler of work, remembered at a very late age that when he was a boy he witnessed his father being berated in public by his boss. The humiliating scene never left him. Imagine yourself, or someone you care for, on the receiving end of an asshole's actions. Always invoke the Golden Rule.

- If you have to ask yourself if you are acting like an asshole, you probably are. Always ask yourself, "Have I done something today that hurt someone and makes them want to get even with me?" If the answer is yes, you need to change. Apologizing is a good place to start.

- The difference between making hard decisions and being an asshole can be a thin one. The difference is all about the execution. Tough decisions based on instinct and thoughtful analysis are understood. Decisions based on crass criteria, rumor or a knee-jerk response will relegate a leader to the sinful category.

- Never gloat, never talk about money in public, and never cease to be honorable, even in difficult situations.

10

REDEMPTION

Rejoice: Hope and Career Resurrection

I once called a candidate for a job early in the morning. Well, not that early to most of the world. It was 9:00 am and he was in college and looking for that great entry-level job. The phone rang in his room and he answered it by saying, "This better be good." Someone should have told him that when you're looking for a job there are good and bad ways to answer the phone.

There are just some things you do and some things you don't—the rules and common-sense behaviors that no one may tell you and are not written down. But if you violate them, you are dinged. The candidate previously mentioned did not get that job. He was not being the CEO of his own career.

The simple things you simply "do" and "don't do" are part of a huge category of information I call "the code of too simple not to know." Call it folklore, call it common sense, call it courtesy, call it using judgment that will help you succeed—just don't call it etiquette. These are the pearls of wisdom that may not have a rationale, may not have a basis in quantitative reasoning, but are vital to success.

Some of them seem so obvious that I wonder why reminders are necessary. For example, why do I have to remind senior executives to wear clothes that fit? That if they wear shirts with their hairy belly sticking out people will notice? Why do people walk around with toothpicks in their mouth? Why do otherwise normal people use their middle finger as a driving tool?

The code addresses any activities that can be regarded as "acting in poor taste." Firing someone through an email message is in poor taste. If that person is pregnant, it is very poor taste.

The code changes and morphs all the time as life and technology evolves. New parts of the code are emerging that deal with iPods, text messaging, American Idol, blogs, and hybrid cars. Since there will never be a written code, it is up to you to always know where the code is moving.

We can all create our own list of what goes on the Not To Do list, from our experience. Remember the boss from Chapter 5 who had a ritual whenever he moved into a new office? His theory was that since he spent so much time there and he felt guilty about it that he wanted the "essence" of his wife there. So on a weekend, he would take her to his office and have sex on his desk. He would announce the ritual to the rest of the staff on the following Monday. His gaffe will forever be on my Not To Do list.

Of course, we can't forget the to-do's from Mom, like Wear Clean Underwear and Keep Your Hands to Yourself. Pay attention to those timeless insights, and look out for new ones as life makes them necessary. Don't expect to read them in any book (except maybe this one).

Violating "the code" reflects especially poorly on a CEO for several reasons. First, how he acts reflects directly on the organization and how it is viewed. Think Larry Ellison at Oracle, think Steve Jobs at Apple, think Mark Zuckerberg at Facebook, to name a few. Secondly, there is just a general sense that the CEO should know the "code." Somewhere along the line every leader should have attended a class on the "code" in CEO school. Alas, some CEOs in the making cut the class. So here is a set of reasons why they should care about the "code."

- **Critical Mass.** For a CEO, sins can pile up. One can lead to another because CEOs are often surrounded by people who don't dare tell the truth.

- **Visibility.** CEOs might be blind to their sins. I hope those who are the most blind receive this book, even if it is anonymously slipped under the corner-office door at night.

- **Geometric Impact.** The sins of a leader can affect thousands of people and communities. He needs to be constantly reminded of this.

- **Clay Feet.** CEOs should know better. Sometimes they don't.

- **CEOs Are Different.** Yes, they are. Some live in worlds we will never know. Some are the guy next door. In all cases, they are full of ambition and the burdens of responsibility that can lead them in bad directions.

- **Choices Abound.** There are choices to be made all the time, and I want CEOs to make the right ones.

WORK HAPPENS BETWEEN EMAILS

So it is written in today's organizations. Between emails, a CEO influences his employees, shapes corporate culture, often earns lots of money, all while carrying the success or failure of the organization on his shoulders. In many instances he may find himself cursed to hell by the very people he is supposed to be leading—when they perceive his sins.

But we can learn from the strengths and weaknesses, the victories and defeats of CEOs and leaders we see every day. Such commitment to observing others, and not sparing ourselves, is this book's biggest takeaway.

The Final Takeaways

We all are fluent in the language of PowerPoint, with headlines followed by bullet points. And, since I am the big believer that so much of what is bantered about in business can be reduced to simple ideas, and since I invented the category of business books that are all bullets, here are the vital few bullet points to summarize attributes that will keep you free of sin.

- **Perspective.** Like the beleaguered communications company leader who claimed, "It's only dial tone," you can draw upon your big-picture insights to set priorities. "The devil is in the details," so don't get derailed on those anthills of sin. Sometimes it's as simple as sitting back in your chair and asking yourself, "What's the most important thing I can do today?" It might be going to your daughter's soccer game and catching up later, or it might be creating the new customer strategy.

- **Honesty.** Examples of deceit like Enron and WorldCom are not as common as we may think. But every day breeds millions of tiny corporate lies that fester like lice or fleas. Sometimes if you "double click" on the truth, on what's right in front of you, your organization will be more successful—or at least will be spared the consequences of small lies gone viral. It might be as simple as asking questions like, "Have we all just agreed to undertake that onerous task?" Or, "Do we *really* think this project will ever be finished?"

- **Awareness.** Wake up. Know what is going on around you. If all of the competitors in your marketplace are staging layoffs, you will be too. If you know you haven't contributed to the success of your organization in a long time, everyone else does too. Be aware of what is important and focus on how you might best contribute. Never lose the awareness that results count more than activity.

- **Delivery.** Conveying a message that you are competent and things will get done is important. The delivery of that message is embedded in all you do and say, and what you wear, and everything else about you. There is no place to hide, and you can never let your guard down. Delivery is about what you will be known for—your brand. Your brand should not smack of sin.

Every day you may choose to learn from examples or not, and to make informed, helpful decisions or not.

The choice is yours. As John F. Kennedy said, "To govern is to choose."

The essential choice we make every day is simple: It's about success and failure. It's about setting priorities and objectives, understanding how to achieve them step by step, and seeing to it that we carry out each step.

A successful life and a rewarding career have everything to do with these all-too-simple choices. It's taken for granted that the big choices are worth the attention they receive. We agonize over them, analyze them, consult with psychics over them, chart them, and—admit it—we all make lists of pros and cons about those big choices. And we should.

Yet, the everyday, seemingly small choices deserve space in the brain too and should not be relegated to the "whatever" dumpster. CEOs do not oversee only mergers and strategy. CEOs are vested even more with creating dynamic, successful organizations to which people are proud to contribute.

The CEOs that institute new industry standards uplift our culture, communities and economies. Some, like Bill Gates and Warren Buffet, have broadened the reach of philanthropy. Confident and constructive CEOs seize the opportunity to improve the quality of collective life. Some of them may not be famous, but I feel heartened to report there's a growing list of them.

I wish all who are in a leadership position well, and I cheer for them. I know their days are polarized between our need for their empathy and our equally strong need for decisive management. As they live in the balance of our passionate hopes and our impossible expectations, I pray they are able to resist sin.

Addendum: How to Fire a CEO

> *Susan was the CEO of a fairly large consulting firm. She was proud and confident of her achievements. The numbers showed the firm was growing like crazy under her direction. The employees were impressed by her leadership and were proud to follow her into "business battle." The Chairman of the Board thought she might be a little reckless and was always offended by her style. What some regarded as confidence the Chairman thought "brash."*
>
> *One day, the Chairman summoned her on very short notice to his office. She dropped everything, hopped on the plane and flew across country for what she thought might be a meeting about an acquisition.*
>
> *She took a limo from the hotel directly to the Chairman's office and when she went take her bag out of the trunk, the limo driver said happily, "No need M'am, I've been instructed to wait for you and take you right back to the airport." She went in, and five minutes later was back out, having been terminated. In effect, she had just been fired by the limo driver.*

Susan would later tell the story of the limo driver with a sense of humor and wonder. She recounts it to colleagues with a ring of "how not to get rid of a leader." She admitted that everyone in the company may have known that she was about to be terminated, except she herself.

The sin Susan may have committed was oblivion to how she was being perceived by her boss, the Chairman. She was probably also unaware—or perhaps too dimly aware—of the politics, events and commotion that were swirling around her. No doubt, there were secret calls among the board: the executive team may have been warned, and there may have even been a search commissioned and replacement candidates interviewed. In all, it can be said that Susan committed the sin of Cluelessness big time.

But what about the Chairman of the Board? Did he need to summon her across the country? What is the best way to fire a leader? Is there a manual out of HR? Is there a particular protocol? Do leaders always know when their days are numbered? Should they?

THERE ARE TWO KINDS OF CEOS: THOSE WHO HAVE BEEN FIRED AND THOSE WHO WILL BE FIRED

Perhaps this old saw about the "two kinds of CEOs" is true. Yet, the protocols for termination are as varied as the personalities of leaders and the style of organizations. In short, one size does not fit all.

Almost always, leaders don't want to step down—and who could blame them? Look at the world news on any given day. Egos are involved. Comfort and benefits are involved. (Who wants to lose the plane?) Fear is involved. (What will I do next? How will I tell my family?) Money is involved in all of its glory as it relates to retirement and benefits. With leaders hoping to sustain their positions as they battle temptations to sin with varying degrees of success, it's no wonder that their turnover creates tension.

A CEO's greatest responsibility is maintaining shareholder value and a favorable public perception of his company. He is generally fired when he fails to accomplish these feats through lapses in judgment, missed performance goals, or even because of the political climate. Other times, there is no good reason besides "time for a change." These are variations on the same reasons we all get fired. But a big difference is that CEOs don't get laid off because of downturns in the business—they create downturns in the business.

An oft repeated phrase among boards of directors is: "the most important thing we do is hire and fire the CEO." Truer words have never been spoken, yet most boards perform both tasks poorly. This is true whether the organization is a multi-national billion dollar corporation or the local not-for-profit.

Still, change is happening in the CEO suite. Increasingly, people recognize that not everyone is suited to the rigors of being a CEO. Boards of directors are making swifter decisions and minimizing their own sins in the process. Short CEO tenure can be a good thing.

And sometimes board members know they must say, "It's not our decision, but you have to go." This occurred at BP when public sentiment against Tony Hayward became overwhelming during the Deepwater Horizon oil spill of 2010. Here is a world class example of Sin by Fibbing: Hayward used expressions like "very, very modest" and "relatively tiny" to describe one of the worst offshore oil spill accidents in history.

Sins do catch up with those who commit them. And with dead bodies paving the way to his demise, a leader should know he's on his way out.

You Just Slip Out the Back, Jack

Most CEO terminations are less tragic—and less inevitable—than those of Hayward, Kenneth Lay and Bernie Madoff. Some, like Susan's, are downright arbitrary. Should you happen to serve on a board of directors, you may find yourself presiding over such a decision. When that fateful day arrives, here are some tips on how to fire your CEO:

- Call him in on Friday afternoon and make sure he brings his badge. Today is his last day and someone will pack up his things later.

- Make life so miserable for him that he quits. Otherwise known as the POW strategy whereby any alternative is better than his current life.

- Establish a three month transition plan. Expect the CEO to play golf the entire time.

- Set the stage for a palace revolt. Do an employee survey knowing full well the answer to the question, "Do you support the CEO?"

- Let him hang himself. Wait until the sins are so heinous that termination is inevitable.

- Send mixed messages: Direct to be more strategic and then drill him for not knowing every single number. Then, either lack of strategy or lack of knowing the numbers are grounds for dismissal.

- Set performance goals year after year that are unreachable. When the goals are never reached, cite lack of performance as the reason.

In all cases, leadership change is traumatic for both the leader (and his family) as well as for the organization. Leaders almost never have a succession strategy. Since they think they are irreplaceable, why bother?

The Kicking and Screaming will Follow

When a CEO is fired, it's a lesson for all of us that sinners do not get off scot free. They get fired just like the rest of us. In fact, leaders are more likely to get fired. The headlines may scream of their hefty severance packages and walking away with big golden parachutes. But CEOs don't like being fired any more than the rest of us.

Once the termination has been announced, CEO resentment will set in immediately. There are those who think they paid their dues and deserve to keep the job, no matter what. They toiled for years and they cannot be fired because, gosh darnit, they earned it.

There are others who, as noted earlier, were lucky in the gene pool and inherited their CEO job. In these cases, they may not get fired until things go belly-up, because they own the place. All in all it is no guarantee of tenure.

Others may actually want to get fired because of a clause in their contract that could enable them to make more money by not showing up than if they resided in the corner cubicle every day. Nice work if you can get it.

How to read the Writing on the Cubicle

None of us should be naïve about what is going on around us in the workplace and we should all listen to our instincts when it comes to job survival. Keep two clues close to heart, regardless of your level in the organization:

- If you are worried about your job, you probably should be. Who knows better than you whether or not you are contributing?

- Still, we're all subjective about our own performance, and may be overly hard on ourselves. If others tell you that you should be worried about your job, you really should be. Who knows better than your co-workers?

Assuming you want to keep your job, follow your instincts and pay attention to how you feel at the office, how people speak to you and about you. While the clues above are not quantifiable, two clear statistics may tell the tale:

- Reduced amount of emails—If you are not being included or asked to contribute, if you are not being informed, you are in trouble. When you turn on your computer and say, "Wow, not too many emails today," you really might be saying, "Why don't I have too many emails today? What's going on here?"

- Lack of Invitations—Not getting invited to meetings? Not getting invited for beers after work? Not going to the trade show in Las Vegas? Not on the panel at the customer forum? Not at the strategy retreat?

Do some counting. If you are seeing emails, memos and invitations diminish, it's time to dust off the resume.

If, on the other hand, you want to get fired—and employees sometimes have good reason to—just check the Employee Manual and do the opposite. Chances are, your settlement won't include the same provisions as a CEO's. For those who might want to expedite termination anyway, here is a short list of tricks you won't find in the Employee Manual:

• Take a weapon to work.

• Say you are bringing a weapon to work.

• Get caught on a video doing something you will regret. As one leader I know said, "What were once memories are now evidence."

• Use the company technology to distribute or view pornography.

• Tell a racist, homophobic or misogynist joke.

• Steal something other than paper clips from the office.

• Make it clear that you are smarter and can do your boss's job better than he can.

WE ARE ALL CEOs

I wish I could tell all readers, whether you're a CEO or employee, that my takeaways will guarantee your job security. But that would be sin by fibbing. I can say with confidence that my suggestions will increase your odds of remaining employed or of being hired elsewhere. I can also say that you'll be more likely to respect yourself and inspire the respect of others.

Exercising self-mastery is crucial, no matter our circumstance. The sins and principles I've discussed apply to a job search and interviews as much as to the daily grind. When we're managing any part of our lives we are CEOs. Everything we undertake presents the opportunity to choose a course of sin or redemption. And the power lies in our choice.

Acknowledgments

No work about organizational life can be complete without the cast of characters that helped make it more interesting. I had the pleasure of working with many who had outstanding senses of humor and would share stories, often with wide eyes and the question: "Is it me or is everyone crazy?" There are too many colleagues to name and thank here, but you will know who you are by the stories I've shared.

Thanks also to the so-called "employees," those who grind it out every day—making sausage or dealing with customers or flying airplanes or writing code. Those employees helped me see things through their eyes and be a better observer. They always tell the truth and I am indebted to them for their insights.

Finally, to Naomi Rosenblatt, my publisher, who saw the candor and humor in the book and brought it out. Thanks.

NOTES:

CPSIA information can be obtained at www.ICGtesting.com
Printed in the USA
BVOW010000131011

273506BV00004B/2/P